Praise for *Trump Bubbles*

"Bill Eddy's latest book, *Tru*  ct
personality analysis into a swee d
the high-risk effect of their persc s
frightening, insightful and hopei ....ing read
about important issues. Narcissistic political leaders are highly
attractive, but also can be very dangerous."

—**JOSEPH BURGO,** PhD, clinical psychologist and author of
*The Narcissist You Know: Defending Yourself Against Extreme
Narcissists in an All-About-Me Age*

"Bill Eddy comes through in the nick of time with this
tremendous exploration of high-conflict personalities in politics.
Whether you are an anxious voter, a citizen who's fed up with
American politics, or someone who's tired of drama in leadership,
this book is for you. Nobody understands the psychological
dynamics of high-profile and high-conflict politicians, or how
to deal with them, better than Eddy. Get this book now, read it,
and apply what's inside. *Trump Bubbles* may be one of the most
significant and needed books of the decade."

—**NATE REGIER,** PhD, CEO of Next Element Consulting
and author of *Beyond Drama: Transcending Energy Vampires* and
*Conflict without Casualties: A Field Guide for Leading
with Compassionate Accountability*

"Picking up on the themes that Bill Eddy and I wrote about
in our book *Splitting America*, published just before the 2012
presidential election, *Trump Bubbles* offers a stimulating, insightful,
and in-depth historic analysis of previous political and economic
'bubbles' that, predictably, have risen and fallen over the years, and
carries us forward into the unsettling 2016 presidential election—
with its worrisome 'Trump phenomenon.' Bill's well-documented
explanation of this phenomenon is fascinating and informative,

as he clearly illustrates the perils for our nation of having a high-conflict person in a major leadership position of power."

—DONALD T. SAPOSNEK, PhD, author of
Mediating Child Custody Disputes: A Strategic Approach and
co-author of *Splitting America: How Politicians, Super PACs and the
News Media Mirror High Conflict Divorce*

"From the rise and fall of Nazi Germany, to McCarthyism, to the Vietnam War and the Iraq War, Eddy points out how political leadership by narcissistic personalities is nothing new. What's new are the recent cultural, economic, and social changes—including American media practices—that have created the perfect storm of American politics in 2016. Eddy offers concrete recommendations on how each of us can respond to 'Trump bubbles' now and in the future. This book should be required reading before voting for any candidate."

—ALISON L. PATTON, Esq., attorney, mediator, and
contributing writer to Huffington Post and lemonadedivorce.com

"No matter where you stand on the politic spectrum, you have a responsibility to read this book. Bill Eddy brings the reality of our world into focus through the lenses of history, psychology, and politics. He gives us all a way to make sense of the high-conflict culture in which we live and offers the long-overdue gift of sound, down-to-earth advice about how to maintain our sanity, if not our civilization. If only *Trump Bubbles* had been in print seventy or eighty years ago, humanity would today be in a far healthier place."

—BENJAMIN D. GARBER, PhD, author of
*Holding Tight/Letting Go, Developmental Psychology for
Family Law Professionals,* and *Keeping Kids Out of the Middle*

TRUMP
BUBBLES

TRUMP BUBBLES

THE DRAMATIC RISE AND FALL OF HIGH-CONFLICT POLITICIANS

BILL EDDY, LCSW, ESQ

UNHOOKED BOOKS
an imprint of High Conflict Institute Press
Scottsdale, Arizona

Copyright © 2016 by Bill Eddy
Unhooked Books, LLC
7701 E. Indian School Rd., Ste. F
Scottsdale, AZ 85251
www.unhookedbooks.com

ISBN: 978-1-936268-10-8
eISBN: 978-1-936268-11-5

Library of Congress Control Number: 2016939285

Cover design by Julian Leon
Interior Layout by Jeffrey Fuller

Printed in the United States of America

Also by Bill Eddy:

Splitting America: How Politicians, Super PACS, and the News Media Mirror High-Conflict Divorce, with Donald Saposnek

It's All Your Fault at Work! Managing Narcissists and Other High-Conflict People, with L. Georgi DiStefano

BIFF: Quick Responses to High-Conflict People, Their Personal Attacks, Hostile Email, and Social Media Meltdowns (Second Edition)

So, What's Your Proposal? Shifting High-Conflict People from Blaming to Problem-Solving in 30 Seconds

It's All Your Fault! 12 Tips for Managing People Who Blame Others for Everything

High Conflict People in Legal Disputes

New Ways for Work Coaching Manual & Workbook: Personal Skills for Productive Relationships, with L. Georgi DiStefano

Don't Alienate the Kids! Raising Resilient Children While Avoiding High Conflict Divorce

Splitting: Protecting Yourself While Divorcing with Borderline or Narcissistic Personality Disorder, with Randi Kreger

Managing High Conflict People in Court

The Future of Family Court

New Ways for Families in Separation and Divorce:
Professional Guidebook
Parent Workbook
Collaborative Parent Workbook
Decision Skills Class Instructor's Manual & Workbook
Pre-Mediation Coaching Manual & Workbook

Dedicated to future leaders everywhere:
May you learn to build bridges and not walls.

CONTENTS

PREFACE

DONALD TRUMP is potentially the most dangerous person in politics since Adolf Hitler. Not because of his
politics (which are ever changing), but because of his personality
(which is never changing).

Trump has a seductive US-against-THEM personality style
that far exceeds any other candidate, Republican or Democrat,
and can inspire violence. Sure, there was Stalin, Idi Amin, Saddam
Hussein, and other ruthless dictators. But Hitler took a cultured
democracy—like ours—and turned it into a hate machine that he
led into World War II.

Can't happen here? There are many *high-conflict* personality
warning signs that say it can. Donald Saposnek and I predicted
some of this in 2012 in our book *Splitting America.*

You might say that the United States in 2016 is completely
different from Germany almost one hundred years ago. After all,
Germany was heavily burdened with paying reparations after losing World War I in 1918, and then the Great Depression made
that all worse. It was people in the lower-middle class who were
most devastated by this. Hitler knew how to manipulate them into
following him—while blaming everyone else.

In the United States, it is predominantly the lower-middle

class who have recently lost jobs, houses, marriages, and worse because of the Great Recession. Many have become Trump's core group of followers. They have felt ignored by both the Democratic and Republican established politicians (the "establishment"). Such resentments can make large groups of people particularly vulnerable to a strong leader who uses high-conflict patterns of speech, as Trump does—and Hitler did.

Hitler's oratory caused his followers to intensely love him and intensely hate Jews, gypsies, communists, homosexuals, and the parliamentary government in Berlin. He pounded on this so intensely at large rallies that people absorbed his messages without thinking. Trump uses similar high-conflict patterns of speech at large rallies to cause his followers to love him and hate Mexicans, Muslims, African Americans, the president, Congress, and even journalists.

Hitler was the first to use modern electronic media to *dominate* people's political thinking. He had radio speeches constantly pumped into people's homes via radio which compelled them to absorb his toxic messages. He held huge rallies and made movies of them, to reach even more people. Images and sounds have a much more powerful impact on the brain than print media, and Hitler's face and his voice were everywhere.

Trump understands that constantly getting his face and voice on TV and radio has a powerful influence on people. His message is not about useful information or his future policies—it's about how big and strong he is and who to hate now. Even if people's lives aren't as bad here and now as in Hitler's Germany, the power of today's all-pervasive media to promote messages of fear and anger is so much stronger.

I believe that Trump has a 50-50 chance of winning the presidential election in November 2016. The high-conflict personality pattern is already in place and, if I'm correct, Trump has only just begun.

But I believe the Donald Trump bubble can be burst. The way party leaders and others expose this high-conflict pattern to voters can make all the difference. If it is explained *respectfully* to potential voters, I think that Trump can be stopped.

I wish I could tell you that "I guarantee it," "it will be a beautiful thing," and "it will be amazing." But that's part of the hot air that keeps the Trump bubble afloat. We don't need more bubbles.

The following is a short book that I first presented over three weeks in March 2016 as a series of twelve blogs. Instead of hot air, I rely on social science, psychology, and history as well as insight from my professional experience dealing with high-conflict personalities and situations. I hope this will help you and those around you to understand the personality dangers of a Donald Trump Presidency.

Bill Eddy
March 27, 2016

INTRODUCTION

HIGH-CONFLICT POLITICIANS

Remember the dot-com bust of 2000? And the housing and stock market bubbles that burst in 2008? For years, people enthusiastically believed that these areas of spectacular growth would never end. The future was incredible and the bubbles were held up by the hot air of enthusiasm without substance. In 1996, then–Federal Reserve chairman Alan Greenspan referred to this as "irrational exuberance."

But these bubbles did burst, causing millions of people to lose their houses, jobs, marriages, self-esteem and more. These spent bubbles still have ripple effects throughout our economy and the political world to this day. They were pumped up by emotions without thinking. We didn't listen to the people who said they were overblown bubbles that couldn't last.

A TRUMP BUBBLE

I define a *trump bubble* as occurring *when emotions trump thinking in politics*. When fear trumps facts. When leader love trumps logic. It could be a politician, a policy, or a war. In 2016, the trump bubble is Donald J. Trump himself—but there are others. His bubble is just more obvious.

Trump's rise has been surprising to almost everyone, including himself. Some people always said he was full of hot air, but now people are taking him seriously. This is common for *high-conflict people (HCPs* for short*)*, who have a narrow (and predictable) way of thinking and behaving. They have an adversarial approach to almost all of their relationships—it's US against THEM. When they get into politics, HCPs build their entire political agenda on US against THEM.

As Dorothy Thompson, an American reporter said in 1931, after interviewing Hitler two years before he took power in Germany: "[Hitler says] The Jews are responsible for everything." She summarized the situation, adding "take the Jews out of Hitler's program, and the whole thing . . . collapses."

By the end of World War II, it became clear that Thompson was right. But throughout the 1920s and 1930s, people thought Hitler was smarter than that and would change his tune once he was in charge. They were wrong.

In an HCP's eyes, people are simply all-good or all-bad, winners or losers. Sometimes, almost inadvertently, they discover a group of people who are so upset that they will follow this US-against-THEM approach wherever the high-conflict person leads them. Unfortunately, HCPs generally have a distorted picture of the world, don't study history or policy, and are more impulsive than most people.

If they are narcissistic HCPs, they see their ignorance and lack of planning as a good thing, because they already are "brilliant," "attractive" and "powerful." They vigorously defend their mistakes without self-reflection or apology, and instead invest all their energy in attacking others (THEM), often over very petty things. This is because their whole lives have been built around their US-against-THEM, attack-and-defend personalities.

ANGRY WITH A BUTTON

In Donald Trump's case, he has tapped into the anger of a significant section of the electorate who feel recently disenfranchised—primarily because of the economic downturns of the last four decades, culminating in the housing and stock market bubble bursts of 2008. These are real problems that have not been addressed sufficiently by either political party. Trump gives his followers the appearance of addressing these issues by leading his followers with anger against the establishment (US against THEM).

While anger can be good for getting attention (and the primary skill of HCPs is getting attention), it can also be dangerous—very dangerous when combined with the strength of the world's only superpower.

Trump would have a finger on the button of the world's most powerful nuclear weapons if he became president of the United States. The risk of such danger needs to be understood, especially since he demonstrates significant warning signs of a high-conflict personality. In this book I will explain the importance of recognizing high-conflict patterns.

PREDICTING THE TRUMP BUBBLE

You might think I'm crazy to have written a book about the rise *and fall* of Donald Trump when he's riding high in March 2016. But I feel quite confident that the pattern of behavior I describe in this book will play out in the same way that it has for so many other high-conflict leaders—in politics and in business. I just don't know the timing of his fall.

Will it be before or after the November presidential elections?

Therefore, I have written this book to be relevant for generations to come, especially because there have been trump bubbles

a fundamental pattern for high-conflict people, because they are preoccupied with blaming others and trying to justify themselves.

HIGH-CONFLICT PEOPLE (HCPS)

The patterns of high-conflict people are *more predictable* than those of the average person, because they are stuck in repeating them. They have a pattern of increasing conflict, rather than reducing or managing it. Most people respond to a conflict with efforts to solve the problem, but high-conflict people respond with actions that grow the problem. They intensify and prolong disputes, involving lots of other people, so that the conflict gets higher and higher. They repeatedly make existing problems worse and totally create some of the conflicts that they claim they're trying to resolve.

I have been observing and teaching others about this pattern for the past fifteen years in my work as a lawyer, therapist, mediator, and trainer of dispute resolution professionals. The pattern is extremely consistent. On the surface, it contains at least the following key characteristics:

1) Preoccupation with blaming others
2) Lots of "all-or-nothing" thinking
3) Intense or unmanaged emotions
4) Extreme behaviors or threats of extreme behavior

CAUTIONARY NOTE: If you recognize this pattern in anyone you know, DON'T tell them—it will make your life a lot worse for months or years to come. Just think about how you can relate to them in a respectful and cautious manner.

People with these characteristics—whom I call high-conflict people—view relationships as inherently adversarial and often charm those close to them, until the HCP turns on them and treats them as their next *target of blame.*

Under the surface, HCPs also have the following three traits, which are associated with personality disorders:

1) Lack of self-awareness (they don't self-reflect)
2) Lack of behavior change (despite strong negative feedback)
3) Belief that problems just happen (always someone else's fault)

However, high-conflict leaders don't necessarily have personality disorders, although they usually display some of these traits.

Being able to recognize these traits in others will help you understand how to deal with HCPs, especially what you *should not do*:

- Don't try to reason with them.
- Don't pressure them to change their behavior.
- Don't angrily imply it's all their fault.

HIGH-CONFLICT LEADERS

When HCPs become leaders, the situation can become quite serious. Their pattern is to involve many other people in their dysfunction:

- *Targets of blame* who become their innocent victims
- *Followers* who become very loyal and attack the leader's targets of blame
- *Negative advocates* who have more credibility and recruit more followers
- *Ambivalent bystanders* who are uncomfortable but keep their distance

This becomes a tragic pattern for everyone. Yet it is avoidable once people recognize it—especially the advocates and the bystanders. But it is also a hidden and deceptive pattern, so that only the trained eye may see it coming.

THE HIGH-CONFLICT BUBBLE

Most people are truly surprised—even shocked—at the sudden and successful rise of a dysfunctional leader. An enthusiastic bubble of emotional energy forms around the HCP leader, sweeping up others based primarily on the person's intense emotions and appearance of power. Yet there is little substance. It is the hot air that fuels the bubble.

Inevitably, the hot air is unsustainable. Reality sets in. Real information comes forward. Targets of blame push back effectively. Negative advocates start abandoning the leader. The bubble deflates, sometimes quite rapidly or dangerously.

HIGH-CONFLICT POLITICIANS

Unfortunately, this tragic high-conflict leadership pattern is most dangerous when it is accompanied by political power—especially in the hands of the head of a government. The reason is that the HCP pattern also includes *splitting people* (dividing them into "US" and "THEM") and *overreaching* (because they can't stop their own aggressive tendencies). These characteristics, when combined with political power, generally lead to violence and eventually to war in one form or another.

Rather than moderating their positions and becoming more reasonable when they get into power, HCPs become *more aggressive*. I've seen this hundreds of times in family, workplace, and legal disputes involving high-conflict individuals.

With that in mind, it's time to get very serious about the risks that face a nation whose leader has a high-conflict personality. And if it's not Donald Trump, it may be someone else, so it's important to understand these patterns in general. They could occur in a Democrat or a Republican—high-conflict personalities know no party or profession.

While these high-conflict patterns of behavior often look ridiculous at the start, they don't end up as a laughing matter. Plus, there are serious problems in the world today that demand serious attention. Trump's followers have many legitimate grievances—they're just pointed in the wrong direction. They do need to be addressed.

IS TRUMP LIKE HITLER?

I am writing this book primarily to educate those who want to understand and defuse trump bubbles—and possibly influence the outcome of the 2016 presidential election.

Is this all that different from the situation in Germany in the 1920s and 1930s during the rise of Adolf Hitler? Didn't they say: "It can't happen here? Not in the country of Beethoven, Bach, and Goethe." They wished they had spoken up earlier. This book is my way of speaking out now. I encourage others to speak up as well when they see a trump bubble forming.

The Trump phenomenon can happen here and it can happen now—unless we learn and teach these patterns. I hope that we can burst the Donald Trump bubble before too much damage is done to our country. Already many people are in denial, insisting that his intensely angry rhetoric is not contagious, does not inspire hatred, and has no connection to the violence surrounding him. They maintain that these are not warning signs of his future behavior.

Once again: High-conflict people do not become more reasonable after they gain power—they become *more* aggressive. These are warning signs if you understand the rise and fall pattern of high-conflict leaders, whether in politics or in business.

BIGGER THAN TRUMP

The problem is bigger than Trump. After fifteen years of studying and teaching about high-conflict personalities, I want to help people gain knowledge to make it harder for the next trump bubble to get started. It's really not that complicated. But there is a little bit of basic brain science involved, which is where we will start. The reporter quoted above on March 11 was accurate:

"The response when a protest breaks out [at a Trump rally] can seem almost **biological**."

PART I

THE RISE

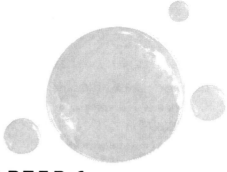

CHAPTER 1

RIGHT-BRAIN POLITICS
(It's All about the Relationship)

"I'm as mad as hell and I'm not going to take this anymore!"
— *Network* (movie), 1976

"[The Republican Party's] most prominent guardians, misunderstanding their own voters, antagonize them as they try to reason with them, driving them even more energetically to Mr. Trump's side."
— M. Barbaro, A. Parker, and J. Martin, *New York Times*

A S DEFINED in the introduction, trump bubbles arise when emotions trump thinking in politics. But how does this occur? Do we have some kind of switch in our brains that can shut off our logical thinking? Can a politician turn off our logical thinking? Can a group?

In 1932, Edgar Mowrer, an American reporter based in Berlin, Germany, asked some young Nazis where they got their extreme beliefs about the Jews:

"Is that logical, is that clear thinking?" [Mowrer asked.]
"*Ach,* thinking!" the exasperated Nazi replied. "We are sick of thinking. Thinking gets you nowhere. The *Fuhrer* himself says true Nazis think with their blood."
And this kind of lack of thinking was everywhere.

EMOTIONS AND LOGIC

The brain has two fundamentally different ways of handling conflict: logical and emotional. The Republican Party leaders referred to in the *New York Times* quote above, Mitt Romney and John McCain, were talking to the "wrong" brain when they said that Trump was a fraud, a phony, and a con artist.

Logical problem-solving (generally associated with the left hemisphere of the brain) involves looking at details, analyzing options, using past solutions to solve today's problems, thinking about policies, planning for the future, using linear thinking, and reasoning with others. The left brain is also where language is mostly processed, so that it lights up with activity (increased blood flow) when we are reading, writing, talking, and listening.

Emotional responses in a conflict are generally associated with the right hemisphere, which can drive intense levels of energy for fighting, fleeing, or freezing to avoid being seen. The right brain takes a big picture perspective, getting a *quick impression* of a situation and running with it, so to speak. Researchers say that the right brain is more focused on relationships—your own and those of others around you—and more actively involved in fast defensive action. It also is most actively involved with creativity, intuition and big-picture thinking.

Because of its relationship emphasis, the right brain is where you pay attention to other people's body language, tone of voice, and facial expressions. "Are you my friend or my enemy?" is the question that the right brain is constantly asking in the background.

Researchers say that most of the time our left brain is dominant. But in a crisis or totally new situation, our right brain instantly takes over. We become focused on fight, flight, or freeze responses, *instead of* analyzing and considering our options. Immediate survival trumps everything else. All-or-nothing solutions.

Don't think—act!

Speed has always been key to survival throughout human history, as we've had to evade predators, large vehicles, and enemies in times of war. No time to think—run! Or fight! While the two sides of the brain have some overlap, with activity occurring in each half almost all the time, the emphasis of each hemisphere seems to be different.

THE AMYGDALA

We even have a part of our brain that is designed to instantly grab our attention away from whatever we were doing: the amygdala. Daniel Goleman, the author of *Emotional Intelligence* (1995) and several related books, suggests that we think of the amygdala as a smoke alarm. It can stop us in our tracks in as few as six milliseconds (six thousandths of a second) or start us running or fighting before we consciously know what we are doing.

Now here's where it gets really interesting: we have *two* amygdalae—one in each hemisphere. The one in your right brain is particularly reactive to facial expressions of fear and anger. This means, if you are busy talking or reading or thinking about something and a person comes into your view with a facial expression of fear or anger, you will become instantly and totally distracted from whatever you were doing!

You will become intently focused on that person and what they are saying or doing. You will get *emotionally hooked* and stop thinking analytically—so you can focus on immediately fighting, fleeing, or freezing in place.

Apparently, the amygdala in your left brain is more reactive to written words.

A LARGER RIGHT AMYGDALA

But now it gets even more interesting, in terms of politics. In 2010, researchers in England at the University College London conducted a study on college students. They had them fill out a questionnaire that helped the students identify politically into five separate groups:

Very Liberal .... Liberal .... Moderate .... Conservative .... Very Conservative

Those who identified as very liberal or very conservative were given brain scans to see if their brains showed any differences related to their political views. The researchers found that the very liberal students had a larger left anterior cingulate cortex, a part of the brain associated with tolerating uncertainty and conflicting information.

On the other hand, the very conservative students had a larger right amygdala. This suggests they were more likely to interpret situations and facial expressions as dangerous. This means they may be predisposed to accepting information that says they are in danger and that they may react more directly to a politician who shows a lot of anger in communicating with them. This also may mean that uncertainty is particularly uncomfortable for them and that expecting or demanding that they tolerate conflicting ideas will not go over very well. They want clear-cut answers and clear-cut action.

FEAR TRUMPS FACTS

Conservatives may actually interpret events as more frightening and angering. When they feel intensely afraid, they may sacrifice logical thought to the more immediate mission of self-defense and survival. Fear without facts. Liberals, on the other hand, may see events as very interesting rather than threatening. Facts without fear.

It appears that we have survived all these years as human beings because we have had both types of brain emphasis in our social groups. Some people specialize in warning us about dangers and others specialize in looking for new solutions to all kinds of problems. One isn't right and the other wrong. We need both conservatives and liberals—and more moderate folks in between.

INBORN OR LEARNED DIFFERENCES?

Are these differences inborn or learned? Moral psychologist Jonathan Haidt has studied and reviewed other research on the difference between liberals and conservatives and found that studies show it is a combination of three things, including nature and nurture, but may start very early in life:

> **Step 1: Genes Make Brains.** . . . Conservatives react more strongly than liberals to signs of danger. . . . Sensation-seeking and openness to experience . . . are among the best-established correlates of liberalism.

> **Step 2: Traits Guide Children Along Different Paths.** . . . One study found that women who called themselves liberals as adults had been rated by their nursery school teachers as having traits consistent with threat insensitivity and novelty-seeking.

> **Step 3: People Construct Life Narratives.** . . . In one study, when asked to account for the development of their own religious faith and moral beliefs, conservatives underscored deep feelings about respect for authority, allegiance to one's group, and purity of the self, whereas liberals emphasized their deep feelings regarding human suffering and social fairness.

Haidt found that both conservatives and liberals hold strong moral values and concerns, but in different ways. Liberals "are more universalistic . . . in the service of underdogs, victims, and powerless groups everywhere. . . . Conservatives, in contrast, are more parochial—concerned about their groups, rather than all of humanity."

OBAMA'S MISTAKE: TALKING TO THE WRONG BRAIN

I thought about this difference soon after the terrorist attacks on citizens in Paris in November 2015, when President Obama gave a speech to the nation. By this time, some conservatives had already expressed strong concern that possible terrorists would enter the United States as Muslim immigrants with all the refugees escaping from the war in Syria.

President Obama became angry and emphasized that the United States is a welcoming country to all people. (The liberal morality.) Unfortunately, he didn't give as much attention to the fears and concerns of conservatives—and much of the nation—about *our citizens* feeling threatened. (The conservative morality.) This was a perfect example of liberals and conservatives both having strong feelings, but about different groups.

Donald Trump understands what very conservative people and very frightened people want to hear. On many occasions, Barack Obama has addressed their concerns as well, but on the night of his speech above, I cringed because I could see the mistake the president was making. Those who are predisposed to feel threats and fear could easily feel abandoned at this peak moment of uncertainty.

TALKING TO THE RIGHT BRAIN

You can see the appeal of a strong leader who views issues in all-or-nothing terms for *our group*. When Trump said he would go beyond waterboarding to provide security for the country, his followers loved it—while most Democrats and most Republican leaders (and most military leaders) were horrified.

So you can also see that, when communicating with people who have right-brain politics, it is beneficial to pay attention to several special features:

1. Relationships, which are a primary concern (the right brain is a relationship brain)
2. Fear, another primary concern (the larger right amygdala)
3. Emotions, as these trump logic under stress (no time for analyzing—fight or flee!)
4. Facial expressions and tone of voice (right brain)
5. Strong desire for certainty (in danger you need to know how to act—now)
6. Resistance to novelty or change (that's a left-brain task)
7. Preference for stories (big picture), rather than facts (no time for details)

In addition, when there appears to be a danger, the right brain automatically switches to fast, defensive thinking, which tends to include several shortcuts from ordinary thinking for the sake of quick, survival action:

8. All-or-nothing thinking
9. Jumping to conclusions
10. Emotional reasoning (it feels true, so it must be true)
11. Personalization (just to be safe, I need to assume they're out to hurt me)
12. Splitting (seeing people as all-good or all-bad—either US or THEM)

All of these characteristics help us understand Trump's appeal to his followers. He is meeting them where they are.

In addition, the right brain appears to be focused on the present, whereas the left brain looks at the past and plans for the future. So when people wonder why Trump supporters can't see the consequences of his personal values and can't see the inconsistencies with his past remarks, the right brain may help explain it. All they can see is the present—danger combined with a leader who looks big and strong.

The right brain is the primary emotional brain and the relationship brain. Putting this in terms of Trump, we can see his appeal to very conservative voters and also why other more reason-oriented Republican leaders don't connect with these voters. They're not recognizing these voters' fears and their need for a reassuring strong relationship with their leaders. Romney has claimed Trump is a fraud and a con artist. But these do not concern Trump's followers—they care about relationship connection, and Trump knows how to connect with his followers. (And Romney doesn't know how to connect with Trump's followers.) Trump cares and Trump is strong; that's the essence of his message.

You can also see that Trump's highly emotional appeal keeps people in their right-brain defensiveness. He constantly tells them they are in danger. It's all about FEAR! He constantly tells them it's an US-against-THEM world today, so you better stick close to me.

He asks them to vote for him, as though they are close friends doing favors for each other. He describes his rallies as "love fests." He needs his followers to feel emotional about him, so that logic doesn't get in the way. Fear without facts. When he tells them that thousands of people in New Jersey were cheering when the World Trade Center buildings were attacked, his followers hear the fear in what he's saying—the facts are irrelevant (and completely untrue say the fact-checkers). He's not a reporter. He's a storyteller. And a very good one for his particular audience.

ROMNEY'S MISTAKE: TALKING TO THE WRONG BRAIN

Trump points out that the Republican establishment can't be trusted—they are part of THEM. He also points out that the news media can't be trusted—they are part of THEM. So whatever the press says about him that's negative can't be trusted. It inspires an angry response instead of insight and concern. He has immunized his followers against the press.

Likewise, when Mitt Romney and other Republican leaders say that Trump's followers are being taken for suckers, they respond with anger rather than careful thought. "How dare you attack our dear leader?"

But why are they so protective of the Donald? Why do they see him as one of US? And why are they so emotional about it? Could this really be like love?

CHAPTER 2

LEADER LOVE
(THE SEDUCTION OF US AGAINST THEM)

(I'm Big and I'm Strong! And I love you!)

"There were those who met Hitler [in the 1920s] and recognized he represented almost a primeval force and possessed an uncanny ability to tap into the emotions and anger of the German people, and those who dismissed him as a clownish figure who would vanish from the political scene as quickly as he had appeared."
—Andrew Nagorski, *Hitlerland: American Eyewitnesses to the Nazi Rise to Power*

"What Trump is doing, then, is showing us something different, something that less fortunate countries know all too well: how authoritarianism works, how it seduces, and ultimately how it wins."
— Ross Douthat, *The New York Times*

WE HAVE JUST looked in chapter 1 at how the emotional right brain can trump the logical left brain when people feel enough fear and anger, and are encouraged to stay afraid and angry. But what makes them follow a particular leader—and commit so loyally to him (or her)?

In Germany, during the 1920s, Hitler was initially seen as a "Little Corporal" and not taken seriously by most Germans. They were particularly angry about the Treaty of Versailles after World War I ended, which required them to pay reparations to France and other countries. But why did they eventually turn to Hitler to save them? Why do people fall in love with high-conflict leaders? How does a trump bubble leader turn off logic and turn on extreme emotions and aggressive actions?

In a recent article, Joshua Rothman describes two different general types of leaders, especially in business: charismatic leaders and bureaucratic leaders. Bureaucratic leaders tend to be process focused, meaning they learn what to *do* in terms of the actions to take to operate the business. Charismatic leaders tend to have powerful personalities and to be skilled at connecting with their followers because of who they *are*.

Ironically, the charismatic CEOs tend to get great publicity, but they also tend to know less, underperform, and get fired more quickly. This is the *rise and fall* (the bubble) that fits closely with the characteristics of narcissistic personalities, who can "talk the talk, but not walk the walk." Yet, Rothman explains that there is a "romance of leadership," according to some research. He says, "When we're swept up in the romance of leadership, we admire leaders who radiate authenticity and authority; we respect and enjoy our 'real' leaders." He continues:

> Our faith in the value of leadership is durable—it survives, again and again, despite our disappointment with actual leaders. Polls suggest that, even though voters who support Trump are frustrated with the people in charge, they aren't disillusioned about leadership in general; they are attracted to Trump's "leadership qualities" and to an authoritarian view of life. In a sense, they're caught in a feedback loop. The glorification of leadership

makes existing leaders seem disappointing by comparison, leading to an ever more desperate search for "real" leaders to replace them.

When I have spoken with followers of Donald Trump, they often mention how "transparent" and "authentic" he is. He "tells it like it is." This is a very appealing quality for those who feel afraid, angry, and mistrustful of other political leaders. Yet it's interesting that, just as with people newly in love, all of the great qualities they describe are qualities that Trump *himself* has told them about himself—not qualities that his followers can actually know or even that others have told them about.

For example, how many people who were once enthralled with O.J. Simpson or Lance Armstrong or Bernie Madoff actually knew that they were living lies *for years?* These were all popular figures with high levels of respect, credibility, and affection at one time—before their bubbles burst in their "fall."

A THEORY OF HIGH-CONFLICT LEADERSHIP

My theory of high-conflict leadership is that it dates back to prehistoric times and is, therefore, "biological." Anthropologists say that we human beings go back about 150,000 years, when we began to have our modern physical and mental capacities. Some research suggests that we have only had spoken language for about 50,000 years and written language for about 5,000 years. This means that, for most of our existence, we humans communicated with each other in nonverbal ways. It also means that we had to get along very well in groups to hunt woolly mammoths or defend against saber-toothed tigers—or other warlike tribes.

In order to work together for survival, we had to have some strong social glue, which probably involved strong leaders that we chose to follow. This would probably have been a more emotional process than a logical one. Because how could someone research a leader's past or know which signs suggested deception versus truthfulness, or whose plans were more realistic?

So instead, early humans had to make judgments based on personal characteristics such as the *appearance of* strength, confidence, charm, interpersonal intensity, and sexual potency. From a present-day standpoint, these types of personal qualities are not logically informative, since we can research someone's past behavior and decisions. Yet our emotions often trump our logic when it comes to love and leadership. The attraction to these traits is based on much more fundamental—and unconscious—forces within us. Clever leaders can call up our yearnings and turn them around for their own purposes without us logically resisting them. It's in their personality DNA and in ours.

Moral psychologist Jonathan Haidt has looked at some of the research on this phenomenon:

> Many political scientists used to assume that people vote selfishly, choosing the candidate or policy that will benefit them the most. But decades of research on public opinion have led to the conclusion that self-interest is a weak predictor of policy preferences. . . .
>
> Rather, people care about their *groups,* whether those be racial, regional, religious, or political. The political scientist Don Kinder summarizes the findings like this: "In matters of public opinion, citizens seem to be asking themselves not 'What's in it for me?' but rather 'What's in it for my group?'" Political opinions function as "badges of social membership.". . . Our politics is groupish, not selfish.

Because of this *groupishness,* when people receive more accurate information from outside the group, it tends to actually reinforce their commitment to the loved leader and to the group rather than pull them away. For example:

> Consider a test of whether apparently credible media corrections alter the belief, supported and pressed by former Alaska governor Sarah Palin, that the Affordable Care Act would create "death panels.". . . But the correction actually backfired among Palin supporters. . . . After receiving the correction, they became *more* likely to believe that the Affordable Care Act contained death panels. Ironically, the correction intensified their original belief. The study suggests that if members of an out-group support some proposition, their very support might entrench the preexisting beliefs of the in-group.

This may help explain why the speech by Republican Party leader Mitt Romney on March 3, 2016, and other Republican leaders' comments, did nothing to pull Trump's "anti-establishment" followers away from him.

To my mind, it seems like his followers are deep in their defensive-protective (right-brain) emotions, so that what they hear is an attack on their dear leader, rather than new information to be considered in terms of logical problem-solving (left brain). When you "try to reason with" people who are stuck in their right-brain defensiveness, you're talking to the wrong brain and only end up reinforcing their defensiveness. This is part of why Trump repeatedly tells his crowds how unfairly he—and they—are being treated by the establishment. This keeps the emotional defensiveness as high as possible, which trumps any logical input.

THE RISE OF HITLER

One of the things that American reporters noted about the rise of Hitler during the 1920s and 1930s was that many Germans had an intensely emotional relationship with him. In 1936, an American correspondent got to ride in a parade behind Hitler's car. He said, "There could be no question about the German people's intoxication with their leader."

And this intoxication made them blind. In 1939, after Hitler had started to invade Europe, another reporter wrote that German newspapers were trumpeting totally misleading headlines saying that these countries were threatening the destruction of Germany. "You ask: But the German people can't possibly believe these lies? Then you talk to them. So many do."

As previously noted, one of the things that Hitler used to inspire people was to hold numerous massive rallies and to make movies of them to show the rest of the country. These were an especially powerful way to give a sense of power and self-esteem to a downtrodden nation after World War I. He kept feeding the group identity and emotions. His followers became fanatical followers.

One frightening thing about what happened with Germany in the 1920s and 1930s is how people in the United States missed the threat that Hitler posed—even the American visitors, celebrities (Charles Lindbergh), industrialists (Henry Ford), and reporters. There was the general belief that the United States should stay out of Europe's business and that Hitler was insignificant. Yet at this very time, he was building absolute loyalty among his growing number of followers as a heroic leader who would save them from their recent history and their declining standard of living after the worldwide stock market crash of 1929.

Yet the issue was, in many ways, not so much economic as it was emotional resentment over their loss of status as a great country. Here's how one correspondent described the average Hitler supporter in 1932, a year before Hitler took power:

> He was male, in his early thirties, a town resident of lower middle-class origin, without high school education;

. . . had no political affiliations before joining the National Socialist party and belonged to no veteran or semi-military organizations. . . . He was strongly dissatisfied with the republican regime in Germany, but had no specific anti-Semitic bias. His economic status was secure, for not once did he have to change his occupation, job, or residence, nor was he ever unemployed.

In other words, the emotions of feeling disrespected by the world, disregarded by his own government (which was fairly immobilized in endless parliamentary conflict), and generally unimportant in his country left him ripe for a leader who seemed to speak to him—even though he wasn't starving or unemployed.

Hitler apparently swept up his followers with inspiring speeches about bringing Germany back from its downtrodden status, as described early in his political career in 1922 by one observer. He noted that "especially the ladies" were enjoying his speech and that one could not tear her eyes away:

> Transfixed as if in some devotional ecstasy, she had ceased to be herself and was completely under the spell of Hitler's despotic faith in **Germany's future greatness**. (Emphasis added)

We now know how out of control this patriotic, self-esteem-building message became. It's interesting to see Trump's hats that say "Make America **Great** Again!" (Emphasis added)

Of course, in the United States in 2016 we don't have the Treaty of Versailles and its requirements to pay expensive reparations to pull us down, followed by the Great Depression. It couldn't happen here, right?

But then again, what about the non-financial issues of deep resentment that so many felt in Germany, such as the average Hitler supporter described above who never lost a job? Why do reporters say that the Trump campaign for president has tapped into a deep anger among his followers? Why, at Trump's raucous rallies, are minorities getting roughed up and the Donald himself saying about one of them: "I feel like punching him in the face!" But on the other hand, his fans seem to love him and his strength. And he loves them back, ending many rallies by saying "I love you! I love you!"

Is there something equivalent happening now in the United States related to the deep resentments of large parts of society? And is there something similar about Trump's skills with our more pervasive modern media that follows the same Hitler playbook? Is the combination of these two phenomena a powerful new threat, given our biological tendency to follow our group over self-interest, and to follow emotion over logic?

CHAPTER 3

THE POWER OF LOSS AND RESENTMENT

(Ripe for US against THEM)

"The intersection of inequality driven by real wage/income stagnation and the fact that the folks perceived to have blown the damn economy up not only recovered first, but got government assistance in the form of bailouts to do so. If you're in the anxious middle and that doesn't deeply piss you off, you're an unusually forgiving person."

—Thomas B. Edsall, quoting Jared Bernstein of the Center for Budget and Policy Priorities explaining "disillusionment with old guard Republicans"

IT WASN'T SO MUCH POVERTY that made Germans ripe for following Hitler—it was resentment over their losses. While they were economically set back by World War I, the lower-middle class was still getting by, as demonstrated by the example at the end of chapter 2 about the average Nazi still having a job in 1932.

But Germans' status was set back in the world from losing WW I, and the lower-middle class was set back in Germany. They could see rich people still having a good time while they were squeezed, especially in the Roaring Twenties that led up to the stock market crash of 1929. They also resented the parliamentary government based in Berlin, which spent all of its time squabbling rather than addressing their needs. This resentment was especially strong in Bavaria in cities such as Nuremberg, where Hitler built the Nazi party and held his largest rallies.

THE DOMINANCE HIERARCHY AND RELATIVE DEPRIVATION

Part of the social DNA of all mammals is a *dominance hierarchy*. We're always struggling to move up individually and collectively in our communities and in the world, and we really resent it when circumstances or our peers knock us down. This is true of dogs, cats, wolves, kangaroos, baboons, and even human beings. And politics is one of the clearest ways that we humans demonstrate this inborn social tendency.

Several years ago I came across the concept of *relative deprivation*. It means that people feel poor primarily because of their circumstances relative to those around them. It's the dominance hierarchy playing out economically. So someone in a big city with a TV set, a cell phone, a car, and a rundown apartment might feel poorer than someone living on a hill in a low-income country with no running water and an outhouse.

For example, several years ago a worldwide review of happiness in different countries rated people in South America as generally happier than they should be for their economic circumstances. But they don't know that they're poor because they're mostly surrounded by people in similar economic conditions.

An American example was Mark Twain (Samuel L. Clemens), the writer of *Tom Sawyer* and many other beloved books. He said he grew up dirt poor along the Mississippi River, but didn't know he was dirt poor—because that's all he knew. Everyone was poor, so no one had a dominance hierarchy issue about it.

FORTY YEARS OF LOSS
AND RESENTMENT

According to a recent *Wall Street Journal* article, until around 1970, Americans saw themselves as a classless country in which anyone could move up and in which people with more money were still one of "US." Most people who became "rich" still identified as middle class and ordinary guys and gals with the same interests and conversations as everyone else.

Since that time, jobs for people without a college education have been diminishing—either taken over by technology, shipped to China, or to a lesser extent taken by minorities and new immigrants for less money. American jobs—and with them, marriages—have declined dramatically for the white working class, especially men. Charles Murray describes the situation in a recent *Wall Street Journal* article:

> For white working-class men in their 30s and 40s— what should be the prime decades for working and raising a family—participation in the labor force dropped from 96% in 1968 to 79% in 2015. Over that same period, the portion of these men who were married dropped from 86% to 52%. . . .

> In today's average white working-class neighborhood, about one out of five men in the prime of life isn't even looking for work; they are living off girlfriends, siblings or parents, on disability, or else subsisting on off-the-books or criminal income. Almost half aren't married, with all the collateral social problems that go with large numbers of unattached males.

At the same time, an upper class has been evolving that sees itself as superior to mainstream Americans. This superiority is clearly felt by what has become the lower-middle class. Murray continues:

> Another characteristic of the new upper class—and something new under the American sun—is their easy acceptance of being members of an upper class and their condescension toward ordinary Americans. . . .

> For its part, mainstream America is fully aware of this condescension and contempt and is understandably irritated by it. American egalitarianism is on its last legs.

In reality, this new upper class represents about 1 percent of Americans, whose income has risen dramatically—generally made up of individuals earning about $400,000 or more per year—while the average income for the rest of nation has been stalled during these same four decades. Since the economic crisis of 2008, the result has been the same, except that the average American is somewhat worse off—some more than others—and the 1 percent has done even better.

RELATIVE DEPRIVATION AND THE TEA PARTY

This setback for the middle class gave rise to the Tea Party, a not-impoverished group, but one driven by those who felt a sense of loss of their own economic future and a loss of the country they once knew. They were especially concerned about the bailout of the banks, which was started by George W. Bush and finished by Barack Obama. The importance of this was recently described by Norm Ornstein of the center-right American Enterprise Institute:

> The widespread sense that all the elites in Washington and New York conspired to bail out the miscreants who caused the disaster and then gave them bonuses, while the

rest of us lost our houses or saw their value, the biggest and often only asset of Americans, plummet, lost our jobs or saw them frozen and stagnant, and then saw gaping inequality grow even more, is just palpable.

But why didn't the Republican middle class blame Wall Street? Why didn't their leaders make an effort to do something to control the "miscreants who caused the disaster"? Perhaps Jared Bernstein (whose words appeared at the beginning of this chapter) helps explain it:

> The core theme of Republican establishment lore has been to demonize not unregulated finance or trade or inequality, but "the other"—e.g., the immigrant or minority taking your job and claiming unneeded government support. And yet, none of their trickle down, deregulatory agenda helped ameliorate the problem at all. So they lost control.

So the Tea Party attempted to take over the Republican Party and actually ran many candidates against the "establishment" who won in the 2010 and 2012 congressional elections. But then Barack Obama also won re-election. His hated "ObamaCare" was upheld by the U.S. Supreme Court. Congress, mostly because of the Tea Party, held votes approximately sixty times to overturn all or part of ObamaCare, but without success.

RESENTING MINORITIES

Perhaps because of the election twice of an African American president, and the failures of the Republican leadership described above, the lower-middle class resentment increasingly became *white* lower-middle-class resentment. Donald Trump was a key player in this when he suggested that Obama was really a foreigner who illegally became president. The "birther" movement was a bubble that rose rapidly and fell just as quickly when Obama finally made his birth certificate public. He was, after all, born to an American mother in the state of Hawaii. Trump's message for years has been that the dominance hierarchy was being threatened by minorities, seeming to say "It must be all their fault your status is slipping."

This raised immigration as a big issue, which focused on illegal immigrants who have come to the United States for decades. The news blared that there are eleven million illegal immigrants from Mexico living in the United States. What the news didn't blare— and I didn't know until I read it—was that this issue is entirely a fictional bubble. As David Brooks writes in the *New York Times*:

> There are more Mexicans leaving the United States than coming in. According to the Pew Research Center, there was a net outflow of 140,000 from 2009 to 2014. If Trump builds his wall, he'll lock more Mexican immigrants in than he'll keep out. . . .
>
> One study of 103 cities between 1994 and 2004 found that violent crime rates decreased as the concentration of immigrants increased. Numerous studies have shown that a big share of the drop in crime rates in the 1990s is a result of the surge in immigration.

THE ONE PERCENT

It wasn't until the Occupy Wall Street movement began in 2011 that most people even became aware there was such growing economic inequality in our nation. The news media never blared this before the Occupy movement. But this movement never became a political movement like the Tea Party. In the election of 2012, Obama was re-elected, but the Republicans took over the Senate largely because of Tea Party conservatives—and big money from the 1 percent! The conservative movement was continuing its rise.

But then by 2014, Obama was gaining confidence and the conservatives were getting nowhere in Congress. The rebellion against the Republican establishment was moving farther to the right again. But I don't believe this was all because of the Republican Party establishment. Another force has been dominating U.S. politics for at least the past twenty years—a force that appeals directly to the "right" brain.

CHAPTER 4

THE POWER OF EMOTIONAL MEDIA

(US against THEM—all day, all the time)

"Liberals and conservatives actually move further apart when they read about research on whether the death penalty deters crime, or when they rate the quality of arguments made by candidates in a presidential debate, or when they evaluate arguments about affirmative action or gun control."

— Jonathan Haidt, *The Righteous Mind: Why Good People are Divided by Politics and Religion*

"Conflict is intrinsically more interesting than consensus. And political conflict has never been more compelling than on Ailes' Fox News. . . . Fox News is as closed off as the media world it proposes to balance—Ailes' audience seldom watches anything else. They have been conditioned by Fox's pundits to see the broadcast networks, CNN, and MSNBC as opponents in a grand partisan struggle."

— Gabriel Sherman, *The Loudest Voice in the Room*

THE RAW EMOTIONS of loss, fear, anger, and resentment can leave an individual overwhelmed and less likely to use critical thinking when it comes to politics. And people whose thinking is already dominated by these strong emotions are very susceptible to being influenced by the emotions and statements of others.

Social scientists talk about "crowd contagion," which can spread very quickly as people share a "single passion" that "leads to united action: collective contagion." Daniel Goleman explains:

> Plays, concerts, and movies all let us enter a shared field of emotions with large numbers of strangers. . . .
>
> Crowd contagion goes on even in the most minimal of groups, three people sitting face to face with each other in silence for a few minutes. In the absence of a power hierarchy, the person with the most emotionally expressive face will set the shared tone.

Remember the concern about Donald Trump's *tone* in the news article in the introduction?

> Despite pre-event disclaimers urging peaceable conduct, Mr. Trump's **tone** often seems to encourage aggression. . . . (Emphasis added)

Modern radio and television have a significant power to influence our emotions through tone of voice and, with television, through facial expression of emotions. They can broadcast an individual's voice and face to millions at the same time. It can also prepare an audience for an emotional leader—even years in advance.

Today's media news is much more about entertainment than about information. Perhaps it has to be, to grab your attention to increase market share in a highly competitive media environment. Television networks compete with each other and with cable network news, all of which compete with online news sources. This makes "news" much more about attention-grabbing extreme emotions and behavior, which can easily trump logical thinking.

THE POWER OF REPETITION

Since your right brain is most sensitive to danger and social drama, media that favors stories of danger and social drama will grab the most attention. And when such stories are repeated and repeated, they get in well below your conscious thought. You become conditioned to their point of view.

Have you ever talked with someone who repeats exactly what someone said on a news program, but they don't even remember where they heard it? Or maybe they thought it was their own original idea! And it may or may not have any actual substance to it. It may all be enthusiastic news without substance—a bubble. But it is nonetheless absorbed as true and repeated and repeated again.

FACE AND VOICE NEWS

Media that speaks the language of the right brain will trump media that speaks the language of the left brain. Thus, face and voice media, such as television and radio, will get more attention than newspapers and books. We have seen the rapid shift to face and voice news just in the last decade, as so many newspapers have gone out of business. Of course, the Internet offers written words as well as face and voice news, but you are seeing the same shift nowadays with streaming video receiving increasingly more attention than written words on the Internet—unless they are very short messages, such as tweets and texts. Otherwise, we focus more and more on pictures and videos from all sources, many of which are repeating each other.

When politics was reported primarily in the newspapers, we had time to think about what we read. The written word is processed primarily in the left hemisphere of the brain, which is more analytical and takes more time to contemplate ideas. With the shift to primarily face and voice media, we have little time to logically "think" about the news and so our reactions are instead dominated by gut feelings—especially fear and anger, which is what sells the most.

Have you noticed that Donald Trump manages to get in the news every day? You hear his voice, if he's on a TV phone interview or calling in on a talk radio show. You see his face almost daily, either at a presidential debate, or days before when people are wondering whether he will attend, or discussing what he said after a debate or a rally. The news media talked about his negative comments to Fox News anchor Megyn Kelly for weeks, often showing a picture of his face when doing so. A strong man challenging a strong media outlet—how exciting!

Today's face and voice news may be ten times more powerful than the radio speeches that Hitler gave, because now they can be repeated over and over again throughout the day and the night for days on end. The news now includes and emphasizes what disrespectful comment politicians, celebrities, and world leaders have said the day before, often with video clips. The worst news makes for the best news.

GROUP NEWS

In chapter 2 we talked about research showing that "Our politics is groupish, not selfish." The *Wall Street Journal* article in chapter 3 also suggested that our culture has shifted to more subgroup identification over the last forty years. Charles Murray, the article's author, suggests that the civil rights movement of the sixties and the feminist movement rightfully demanded their place in America, but that the new push for affirmative action "demanded that people be treated as groups" now rather than individuals in one group—the nation.

Consequently, in our modern technological age, it's not surprising that news has also become group oriented—and group isolated. We have many options for media, so we gravitate toward those that offer points of view similar to our own. In the "old" days when most people watched Walter Cronkite host the evening news, he decided what was newsworthy and everyone watched his choices. There was a sense of unity in the country—one nation, one view of the world—that is not possible now, with so many choices. The proliferation of choices also brings new competition as each news channel has to aggressively grab our attention to get us to watch at all.

In this media environment, we develop a sense of identity and community around our favorite shows, including the news. How do you get your news? Who do you watch or listen to? Are you open to other points of view? And how do you separate news from opinion? Today's top-rated news shows are actually opinion shows—on Fox News.

THE US-AGAINST-THEM NEWS CHANNELS

With the advent of cable networks, political talk has exploded since the 1990s. And with the end of the Fairness Doctrine in 1987, television news can be totally one-sided politically. (See our discussion of this in Eddy, B. and Saposnek, D. *Splitting America.* 2012, Scottsdale, AZ: Unhooked Books.)

In 1996, two new cable news channels were started, MSNBC and Fox News—one left leaning (MSNBC) and the other right leaning (Fox). Over time both tipped more and more heavily in their own direction. Remember the increasing effect of groupishness?

However, Fox has been much more successful than all the other channels. I would argue that it's because "right brain" news trumps "left brain" news. In other words, news that focuses on fear and anger will trump news that focuses on ideas and a variety of points of view.

No one understands US-against-THEM news that grabs your attention better than Roger Ailes, who founded Fox News. Here's how author Gabriel Sherman describes Ailes:

> As a pugnacious television adviser to Presidents Nixon, Ronald Reagan, and George H. W. Bush and then as the progenitor of Fox News, Ailes remade both American politics and media. More than anyone of his generation, he helped transform politics into mass entertainment—monetizing the politics while making entertainment a potent organizing force. "Politics is power, and communications is power," he said after the 1968 election. Through Fox, Ailes helped polarize the American electorate, drawing sharp, with-us-or-against-us lines, demonizing foes, preaching against compromise.

Ailes was a Republican adviser who hoped to use Fox to stem the tide of mainstream media and liberal politics. He viewed television as having more power to influence political thinking in America than helping presidents get elected. His approach has been so successful that he has had a tremendous impact on all major news reporting.

By 2002, Fox was the number one cable news network. Its audience soon "more than doubled that of CNN and MSNBC, and its profits were believed to exceed those of its cable news rivals and the broadcast evening newscasts *combined*."

Ailes made news sexy, with young blond reporters who wore tight blouses and sat at glass desktops so you could see their legs. He made the programming dramatic. And he filled it with conservative opinion-makers. The other network news programs have adopted some of his style in the newsroom, and they often repeat dramatic stories that first air on Fox. They also now replay stories from conservative radio commentator Rush Limbaugh (voice news) and even show clips of him during TV network news programs talking to his radio listeners. All of this has created a powerful "echo chamber" for conservatives, built significantly on US-against-THEM reporting.

DRAMATIC NEWS COVERAGE

But Roger Ailes may not have grasped the full impact of turning politics into entertainment, based on an intensely repetitious US-against-THEM model. Inadvertently, his Fox News may be driving the Republican Party over a cliff.

The problem he didn't account for is that the brain gets desensitized to danger or drama when we're watching it from a safe distance. Therefore, danger and drama in a passive medium, such as television, must continually escalate in order to keep grabbing our attention—much as an addict craves more and more.

Slowly, with this escalating news, the entertainment has separated itself from the information—it has become more and more of a bubble of enthusiasm without substance. There's no clearer example of this than what happened with news coverage of the Affordable Care Act.

Many Democrats wanted a single-payer system, but the ACA adopted a Republican compromise model that had been raised in the 1990s. It was very similar to the system that Massachusetts adopted under Governor Mitt Romney, although he vigorously denied that in order to get nominated by the Republican Party in 2012.

Most of the work on the ACA was done during Barack Obama's first year as president in 2009. When the August congressional break came, senators and representatives went home to their constituents and many of them held community meetings to discuss the ACA. Most voters knew little about the proposed health-care plan and listened patiently to hear from their representatives. At a few of these meetings, some citizens shouted at their representatives that they didn't want to change anything. Sherman explains:

Now Obama advisers were getting word that Fox was actively manipulating the coverage of the health care debate, which at the time was being played out in a national series of town halls. "We had anecdotal reports that where there was no screaming, they would not report it." . . .

What most alarmed the White House was that the rest of the media was suddenly following Fox News's lead. In an interview posted on the *New York Times* website, the paper's managing editor, Jill Abramson, acknowledged that they would need to follow Fox's reporting in the future. "The narrative was being hijacked by Fox," Dunn said. "Fox had taken over a thought-leader role in the national press corps."

So this "shouting news" was repeated and repeated by all the major media. The ACA quickly became *Obamacare* and the hatred for it grew and grew through enthusiastic repetition rather than substantial discussions. Emotional crowd contagion. To this day, few people really know much about Obamacare, but Fox News fans know they hate it and get the impression that it's a disaster and that most of the nation hates it as well.

But that's not true. The Supreme Court upheld the Affordable Care Act/Obamacare. The answer has been to hate the conservative Chief Justice John Roberts, who put forward the tie-breaking vote. Fox News viewers have been told it's a job-killer, but that's not true either. Millions of jobs have been added to the economy since it took effect in 2010. "Hatred for Obamacare" is another bubble that is slowly deflating as it becomes the successful Affordable Care Act.

But if you remember the losses and resentments described in the previous chapter, you know that followers of the Tea Party and other conservative members of Congress have continued to focus their rage against Obama and Obamacare—based on emotion rather than fact. Fox News has played a leading role in pumping up this bubble.

Senator Ted Cruz, a 2016 presidential candidate, led the shutdown of the federal government a few years ago to put a stop to Obamacare, without success. It was a bubble with lots of enthusiasm but little substance. The bubble is now deflating across the United States—replaced by new bubbles of enthusiasm without substance on other subjects.

CONSERVATIVES NOW EATING THEIR OWN

Since 2010, Roger Ailes has wanted to elect a Republican President. Over time he interviewed most of the potential Republican candidates—and hired a lot of them as commentators. However, he didn't give them much attention if, in his eyes, they weren't conservative enough. Take Jon Huntsman, for example, a generally well-respected Republican who believed in global warming and ran for president in 2012. Sherman writes:

> In a meeting at Fox News, Ailes flatly told Huntsman, "You're not of our orthodoxy," citing his stance on climate change. . . . .After finishing third in the New Hampshire primary, Huntsman dropped out of the race. Over the course of his candidacy, he had only banked four hours and thirty-two minutes of Fox face time. By comparison, pizza mogul Herman Cain, who was a candidate for a similar length of time, notched eleven hours and six minutes.

YGMOWYPAT

As the two quotes that open this chapter indicate, liberals and conservatives move farther apart the more they talk to people in their own group. This reminds me of a principle I learned long ago in behavioral psychology: "You get more of what you pay attention to." YGMOWYPAT. (I pronounce this "ig-mowy-pat.") With this in mind, it makes sense that the most popular conservative source of news would grow increasingly conservative over time. As Ailes hosted numerous Republican debates, his candidates became more and more entertaining and less and less grounded in substance.

To prove they are more purely conservative, commentators and candidates end up turning some of the US of yesterday (like Huntsman) into the THEM of today—who they now attack repeatedly, such as in the endless debates. Thus, to survive, conservatives have to keep eating their own in the attention-getting quest for ever more pure politics.

This has been exemplified over the past few months as candidates Chris Christie, Marco Rubio, Cruz, and Trump in particular all tried to outdo each other in showing how conservative they were—attacking each other more and more personally along the way. But ironically, the three who were elected to office as conservatives found themselves treated as part of THEM by Trump, who could claim he was the only one who was totally an "outsider." Now political experience is a liability rather than a plus?

As this process shows, political positions and opinions become more and more separated from reality and enter a fictional zone of politics that creates bubble after bubble of fear and anger without reason, which gets repeated ad nauseam by the all-pervasive news and believed by those who are already afraid and angry. (See chapter 3: The Power of Loss and Resentment.)

ANTIPOLITICS

The moderate-conservative commentator David Brooks criticizes and explains this dynamic, especially when extremely conservative politicians have been elected and fail to perform:

Over the past generation we have seen the rise of a group of people who are against politics. These groups—best exemplified by the Tea Party but not exclusive to the right—want to elect people who have no political experience. They want "outsiders." They delegitimize compromise and deal-making. . . . They suffer from a form of political narcissism, in which they don't accept the legitimacy of other interests and opinions. . . . This antipolitics tendency has had a wretched effect on our democracy. It has led to a series of overlapping downward spirals:

The antipolitics people elect legislators who have no political skills or experience. That incompetence leads to dysfunctional government, which leads to more disgust with government, which leads to a demand for even more outsiders. . . . They make soaring promises and ridiculous expectations. When those expectations are not met, voters grow cynical and, disgusted, turn even further in the direction of antipolitics.

I believe that the escalating drama of US-against-THEM news combined with this downward spiral of ineffective elected conservatives may be why we have Donald Trump today, the ultimate "outsider." It's become a self-fulfilling prophesy of failure and anger—ever more extreme.

THE DEPRESSING NEWS

There is another impact that all-pervasive extremely negative news can have on its viewers: depression, illness, and death. A new study reported by economists Anne Case and Angus Deaton in December 2015 shows that whites ages forty-five to fifty-four without college education have been experiencing an increase in death rates since 1999. At the same time, death rates for similar-age African

Americans and Hispanics have been decreasing. What's going on?

Andrew J. Cherlin, a sociologist at Johns Hopkins University, believes it has to do with "reference theory," which is similar to relative deprivation that I described in chapter 3:

> Why are whites overdosing or drinking themselves to death at higher rates than African-Americans and Hispanics in similar circumstances? Some observers have suggested that higher rates of chronic opioid prescriptions could be involved, along with whites' greater pessimism about their finances. . . .
>
> National surveys show striking racial and ethnic differences in satisfaction with one's social standing relative to one's parents. The General Social Survey conducted by the research organization NORC at the University of Chicago has asked Americans in its biennial surveys to compare their standard of living to that of their parents. In 2014, according to my analysis, among 25-54-year-olds without college degrees, blacks and Hispanics were much more positive than whites: 67 percent of African-Americans and 68 percent of Hispanics responded "much better" or "somewhat better," compared with 47 percent of whites.
>
> Those figures represent a reversal from 2000, when whites were more positive than blacks, 64 percent to 60 percent. (Hispanics were the most positive in nearly all years.) . . .
>
> Reference group theory explains why people who have more may feel they have less. . . . In the fourth quarter of 2015, the median weekly earnings of white men aged 25-54 were $950, well above the same figure for black men ($703) and Hispanic men ($701).

This surprising information seems to parallel the rise of constant news that the white middle class—especially the white lower-middle class without college education—has been a victim of minorities. Whites are still doing better, but the face and voice news doesn't say that. The implied message is that minorities are moving above whites in the dominance hierarchy.

Ironically, the election and re-election of Barack Obama has reinforced this news. The conservative news implies that minorities are getting superior treatment—that they've passed whites. While this isn't supported in fact, the constant talk news bubble keeps it in the air.

The power of resentment, plus the power of face and voice media, makes a substantial part of the voting population even more ripe for an US-against-THEM leader. After being told for twenty years that they are victims, they are ready for someone to tell them who to blame.

CHAPTER 5

THE POWER OF PERSONALITY

(You're with US or you're against US)

"The crowd went wild. In the space of a few minutes, Hitler's rhetoric had won the approval of much of the Munich establishment, including those who only moments before had dismissed him as a half-baked caudillo. "It was an oratorical masterpiece. . . . He swung the temper of the crowd with just a few sentences. It was like turning a glove inside out. Hitler left the hall with the total endorsement of the gathering."
—Peter Ross Range, *1924: The Year That Made Hitler*

THERE ARE TIMES in history when someone is in the right place at the right time to turn the course of human events, for better or for worse. Is Donald Trump one such person?

This book began by talking about high-conflict personalities—people with four key characteristics:

Preoccupation with blaming others

Lots of all-or-nothing thinking

Intense or unmanaged emotions

Extreme behaviors or threats of extreme behaviors

THE THREE KEY INGREDIENTS

Imagine if someone with these characteristics had an *extreme* high-conflict personality—like Hitler. Could that person sway a crowd, any crowd? At any time? Probably not. The circumstances would have to be just right, such as the combination of ingredients we have just put together in this book:

Extreme resentment: The people would have to be very afraid and resentful because of an extreme triggering event.

Extreme emotional media: The media would have to reach far and wide, be extremely repetitive, adversarial, and emphasize voices and faces showing fear and anger.

Extreme high-conflict personality: Someone would have to focus people's existing fears, resentments, and prejudices into action against a specific target of blame—a specific person or group.

Hitler had all three of these ingredients working for him.

RESENTMENT

Hitler started out in the 1920s with a local group of people who were very afraid and angry. But by 1928, the Nazi party had gained only 12 seats in the parliamentary elections, with only 800,000 Germans voting for them.

Then the stock market crashed in 1929. The Nazis won 107 of the 577 seats in the parliament in 1930, with nearly 6.5 million people voting for them. In 1932, the Nazis won 230 seats, making them the largest party in the parliament. There's your extreme resentment based on a triggering event and the voting power of resentment.

EMOTIONAL MEDIA

Hitler was one of the first (if not *the first*) politicians to speak directly to the people on a large scale. Most politicians were boring and had little interest in speaking directly to the people, except for an occasional campaign speech to a gathered crowd. Yet his voice was in almost every home on the radio and his angry face was in the newsreel movies shown far and wide. A seductive dictator would be able to harness this electronic media power and multiply it many times.

HIGH-CONFLICT PERSONALITY

But what if the resentment and the media were the same, but it wasn't Hitler who came along, but another authoritarian personality? Were Germany's actions inevitable regardless of the person?

Here's what was said about Hitler, after studying the news reports and personal correspondence of Americans in Germany in the 1920s and 1930s:

> Their experiences and observations strongly suggest that, without Hitler, the Nazis never would have succeeded in their drive for absolute power. The country still might have embarked on an authoritarian course, possibly a military dictatorship. But whatever might have emerged would not have been on the terrifying scale of the Third Reich, with all its terrifying consequences.

> Even those Americans who initially dismissed the Nazi leader as a clownish figure came to recognize that he possessed an uncanny ability to mesmerize his followers and attract new ones. **He knew how to tap into his countrymen's worst instincts by playing on their fears, resentments and prejudices more masterfully than anyone else.**

(Emphasis in **bold** added for later discussion)

THE THREE KEY INGREDIENTS IN THE UNITED STATES?

Do you think we have these same three ingredients in the United States right now?

RESENTMENT

As chapter 3 explained, a significant part of the lower-middle class has suffered tremendously from the housing and stock market bubbles bursting in 2008. Then there is the additional resentment of seeing those below them in the dominance hierarchy getting assistance from the government, such as with ObamaCare, and those at the top of the hierarchy getting assistance from the government in the bank bailouts. The people are afraid and angry. Does it compare to Germany in the 1920s and 1930s?

Remember, *relative deprivation* and *reference theory* are based on people's *perceptions* and *comparisons*, not the realities of their economic circumstances. Therefore, even though the economic realities for Germans were worse in the 1930s, it's possible that Trump supporters in 2016 have a similar level of resentment for the Great Recession that Germans had for the Great Depression.

EMOTIONAL MEDIA

As explained in chapter 4, today's news media far exceeds the capacity of the radio and movie newsreels of Hitler's day. Now the 24/7 cable news, the Internet repetition of news at everyone's desk, and the "echo chamber" of adversarial news channels hammer us with highlights and updates on the presidential race—and have done so for over a year, with months to go as of March 2016! In this environment, the potential influence of a powerful personality is huge. We're already seeing this in the election coverage. Trump gets much more time to spread his face and voice compared to any other candidate, Democrat or Republican, and his message fits well with the predominant news channel—Fox News.

Plus, with Twitter he can reach his audience directly. In comparing his current success to his earlier failed presidential bids, one journalist, Jill Lepore, wrote:

A lot of Trump's momentum this time around has been fueled by the public-opinion polling industry and by a communications revolution. This election season, there are more polls, and earlier polls, and they are both less reliable than ever before and more influential; meanwhile, Trump has been doing with Twitter what he could not do with a URL. In 1999, he couldn't override the opinions of the political establishment; he couldn't shout it down. Without a direct link to his audience, he couldn't even effectively counter his critics.

Now he has direct, free media coverage—so much more of this ingredient than Hitler had.

HIGH-CONFLICT PERSONALITY

Does Trump have an extreme high-conflict personality? Only time will tell if he can take over the country based on the other two ingredients. I'm writing this book because I hope that he won't. But I believe he is much more of a danger than most people think, for the reasons I'm explaining here. There are more similarities than differences, as follows.

Narcissistic Personality

If you put "Trump Narcissistic Personality Disorder" in a Google search, you get about 169,000 results. If you put "Hitler Narcissistic Personality Disorder" in, you get about 182,000 results. All this shows is that a lot of people are writing about these subjects. But many people ask me what I think about Trump's personality, and I can't say anything about diagnosing him with a personality disorder because I am a licensed mental health professional and shouldn't diagnose someone I have never met.

Therefore, I just don't know. But I will tell you some of the signs of narcissistic personality disorder, and you can draw your own conclusions. This list is drawn from the diagnostic manual of mental disorders used by most mental health professionals and published by the American Psychiatric Association.

To me, the key issue is not whether he actually has a "disorder" but rather a personality pattern of behavior that helps us so we can make some predictions about his future behavior and stability. People with personality disorders or lesser traits are more predictable than others because they have a narrower range of behaviors. This is because of their lack of self-awareness and lack of change that I mentioned in the introduction to this book.

Traits of Narcissistic Personality Disorder

Mental health professionals consider the following general categories of information when assessing whether a patient has such a disorder. While just seeing this list does not tell you very much, it does give you some idea of the self-sabotaging issues such a person *might have.*

Grandiose
Fantasies of power
Believes he's special
Requires admiration
Entitlement
Exploits others
Lacks empathy
Envious
Arrogant

Some of these dynamics suggest how a politician with such traits might act. One tool for measuring narcissism is the Narcissistic Personality Inventory (NPI). Here's how one author interprets these characteristics:

> [I]ndividuals with high NPI scores are highly invested in promoting their self-perceived superiority and are hypervigilant toward detecting and trying to diffuse

potential threats to their grandiose self-perception. . . .

[T]he grandiose and vulnerable aspects of narcissism [suggest] that while narcissists possess an overtly, highly positive sense of self, they also simultaneously possess a covertly fragile and vulnerable sense of self making them constantly dependent on obtaining validation and affirmation from their social environment and interpersonal relationships.

In other words, someone with narcissistic traits might unconsciously be driven to spend all of their time excessively promoting their grandiose side, so that no one can see their vulnerable side. This would also mean they would be "hypervigilant toward detecting and trying to defuse potential threats," which might explain why a narcissist might respond to a challenge (like a direct question challenging his superiority) with a personal attack (like Trump did with Megyn Kelly).

Cautionary note: Resist the temptation to "diagnose" people around you—or yourself—with this disorder, and especially resist the urge to tell people you think they have this disorder. If they do, they will punish you by making your life miserable for months or years to come. If they don't have this disorder, they still won't like your suggesting that they do. It doesn't really matter anyway, because you can still decide to vote against someone whether he or she has this specific problem or not.

Possible Predictions about Narcissists
If Trump does have some of these traits or an actual disorder, then we might make some of the following predictions about his future behavior. Since he is running for the most powerful office in the world, it's reasonable to consider just hints of these problems as a good reason to avoid giving him this power. The concept of "angry with a button" takes on new meaning when you look at how these psychological dynamics work and how dangerous they could be-

come when combined with political power.

Also, keep in mind that knowing about these predictable patterns of behavior is more important than watching someone on television in a debate—or even twenty debates. In a debate, people with these traits usually cover them up well. (It can take six months to a year in a close relationship before you can clearly see that the person may have a pattern of personality-disordered behavior that will lead to serious trouble.)

Here is a list of predictions I recently made for an article from observations of this personality type over the past fifteen years in family and workplace relationships. Narcissists will:

Be very charming—to everyone, not just you; you will not be special to them for long

Be self-absorbed, talking constantly about themselves and paying little or no attention to you

See themselves as constantly victimized by others and constantly tell you about how unfairly they've been treated

Be sore losers, never admitting a loss, finding someone else to blame for any setback

Engage in lawsuits, spreading rumors or even violence against any person who caused them to have a "narcissistic injury" exposing their imperfections or diverting attention from them

Have a drive to be the group leader, or at least the center of group attention

Not work hard, take credit for others' work, and quit if they don't get lots of respect

Increasingly insult you in relationships, including in front of others

Demand your constant admiration. When that fades, look
elsewhere for others to give them fresh new absolute
admiration, then deny they are doing that so they can
keep your admiration active too (such as having multiple
affairs during a marriage, but still keeping the marriage)

At some point lose interest in you and possibly forget that
you ever existed

Does any of this fit Trump? These are just very general predictions about anyone with narcissistic personality traits. We'll see if Trump fulfilled any of them by November, if not sooner.

LEADERSHIP AND MANIPULATION

Regardless of narcissism, one leadership expert, Nate Regier, notes six specific traits that Trump exhibits that violate positive leadership qualities:

Oversimplify and Repeat
Oversimplifying complex issues invites people to think less, and respond more from their emotions, especially fear. Trump is a master of oversimplifying. "I'm going to build a wall and Mexico is going to pay for it," is the oversimplified statement. The more complex version is, "I will reduce our trade deficit with Mexico by $10 billion, and use that extra revenue to pay for the wall." The first statement invites strong emotional responses and polarization without meaningful dialogue, the second invites people to think. . . .

Discount Others' Reality
Manipulation relies on the other person questioning their perception of reality. . . . Trump's version. "Nobody listens to you." "Believe it or not, I'm more presidential than anyone except Abe Lincoln." These phrases are insidious and powerful. The first one was aimed at a reporter. It was a personal attack

aimed at discrediting him and getting the rest of us to believe his perspective was worthless. The second one, used frequently whenever someone questions Trump's behavior, invites others to question their knowledge. . . .

Interrupt

Interrupting is a classic manipulation technique because it is a coercive show of force to exert dominance. The most important outcome of interruption is that it stops any dialogue that challenges the manipulator's position or questions their authority. . . .

Take Credit, Avoid Responsibility

One way to increase my negative influence on another person is to convince them that all the good things are because of me, and all the bad things are because of someone else. The recent rioting and protesting surrounding Trump rallies illustrates how this works. Trump's incendiary rhetoric, especially the use of the *Oversimplify and Repeat* tactic, has stoked major anger and polarization, yet he avoids any responsibility for this. . . .

Turn the Tables

. . . Trump is a Promoter Personality Type, who is gifted with adaptability, charm, and persuasiveness. Highly charismatic, by nature, they are tremendous deal-makers and negotiators. They roll with the punches and their agility can help them be quite successful. On the dark side, when they aren't in a healthy space, they are just as adept at turning the tables on others, out of vengeance. . . . Note how frequently Trump, when pushed to explain himself or accused of negative behavior, will avoid answering the question and instead re-accuse the other person of the exact same thing.

The End Justifies the Means

Manipulators are driven by a narcissistic need to dominate and be the center of everyone's universe. For this reason, any means necessary to achieve this goal is justified. Whenever questioned about his behavior or motives, Trump's most common response is to point to the polls, as if approval from others makes it OK. *"If the polls like me, then what I'm doing is OK."* In the corporate world, a common variation of this is, *"You can't argue with results,"* as a way to justify unethical or adversarial tactics to achieve a goal. **Positive Leadership Lesson:** While great leaders care deeply about having happy followers, they start with a solid, ethical core and know that popularity is not the measure of success.

All of these leadership issues raised by Regier seem to fit well with the "grandiose and vulnerable" sides' theory of narcissistic personalities.

PUBLIC PERSUASION

If Donald Trump has some of these personality traits, then he would lack the flexibility and self-awareness necessary to cope with national and world events as a president. He might become highly resentful that a world leader insulted him, or he might trigger an international incident by off-handedly insulting a world leader. Insults are already a central characteristic of Trump's campaign style. Writer Jill Lepore recounts some of the things he had to say about other countries during his 2000 presidential campaign:

His foreign-policy plans included insulting France ("a terrible partner"), Germany ("they failed militarily"), Japan ("ripping us big-league"), and Saudi Arabia ("I mean, the money they make"). He said that, as President, he would serve as the U.S. trade representative. "Our trading partners would have to negotiate across the table with Donald Trump," he said on Fox News, "and I guarantee you, the rip-off of the United States would end."

On the other hand, people with these traits can be extremely seductive and shower praise and gifts on others in order to get what they want from them.

But could someone's personality and speaking ability turn a whole country in a negative direction? Could Donald Trump be such a person? If you look at his speaking style, it's all about intense emotions and nothing about facts or realistic plans. He has five narrow emotional themes with lots of repetition, which may explain his trump bubble—pure emotions without thinking:

Fear: He tells his crowd they should be very afraid of Mexicans, Muslims, refugees from the Middle East, African Americans, the Chinese, and others.

Anger: He displays anger all the time and gets the crowd to express its anger too. He especially encourages anger at the "Republican establishment," at the existing president and Congress, and at journalists (who provide facts about him that challenge the fantasies he creates).

Love: He repeatedly tells the audience he loves them. "I love you! I love you!" He calls their rallies "love fests."

Strength: He usually starts his rallies with talking about his high poll numbers, but he also brags about his money, his smart brain, his sexual potency.

Energy: He has boundless energy and really seems to enjoy the attention he gets from his crowds.

Interestingly, here's what the director of content at dictionary.com said when interviewed about the words the presidential candidates used in 2016:

> "Bernie [Sanders] and Hillary [Clinton] tend to use concrete language," she explained, "whereas the Republican contenders—with the possible exception of

Kasich—tend to use descriptive language. I think that's partly why Trump's speech is so resonant with his supporters: he's speaking to them on an emotional plane."

This emphasis on intense emotions helps explain Trump's unique ability to instill such intense loyalty in his followers, far beyond what any other candidate we have seen in decades has been able to do. His trump bubble is based on such intense emotions that thinking stops.

If you were to watch him at a rally, in a debate, or being interviewed on a news program, you might keep track of how much of the time he spends on the above emotional messages and how much he spends discussing real facts and proposals.

In reality, he avoids logical discussions and blocks others who attempt to ask reasonable questions. For example, consider the parent asking about swearing described in the introduction of this book and his scathing criticism of Megyn Kelly for asking him a question about disparaging women at a debate. He turns such questions into personal attacks and avoids providing any actual factual information. (Did you notice that his intense emotional appeals above spell FALSE?)

FORCE OF PERSONALITY

The net result is that by sheer force of personality he is able to keep the trump bubble up in the air and to keep US intensely focused on blaming THEM (all of his targets of blame) and not on solving real problems. The question is whether this approach can be applied intensely enough to persuade 50.1 percent of the country to vote for him as president in November 2016.

Let's remember what Americans in Germany said about Hitler at the beginning of this chapter:

> He knew how to tap into his countrymen's worst instincts by playing on their fears, resentments and preju-

dices more masterfully than anyone else.

. . . He possessed an uncanny ability to mesmerize his followers **and attract new ones.** (Emphasis added)

. . . .

CHAPTER 6

SPLITTING AMERICA IN HALF

(Everyone Becomes Angry; Some Become Violent)

"Splitting is unconscious and contagious—just like the effects of advertising. It gets past your radar and you come to believe it unless you realize what is happening. The reason is that high-conflict emotions are highly contagious. If you're in a high-conflict emotional environment, you will "catch" this splitting tendency and start to view people as all-good or all-bad, as well. Children are especially vulnerable to absorbing splitting, but adults do as well—especially in high-conflict divorce and, as we are now seeing, in high-conflict politics."

—Bill Eddy and Don Saposnek, *Splitting America: How Politicians, Super PACs and the News Media Mirror High Conflict Divorce*

"SPLITTING" IS ONE OF the most interesting and surprising (but predictable) dynamics that occurs when someone in a group has a high-conflict personality. This dynamic is most familiar to mental health professionals who see it as a common symptom of borderline and narcissistic personality disorders.

It is a psychological defense mechanism in which the person truly views some people as all-bad and others as all-good. It can usually be traced back to early childhood before youngsters start learning that people have a mix of positive and negative qualities. When there is a problem, people cope by seeing themselves as perfect and others as totally bad.

This defense helps an abused child, for example, avoid feeling the intolerable sadness, guilt, or fear of the consequences of having done something wrong, or being a bad person, or having an incompetent parent (it must be all someone else's fault). By five or six, most children have outgrown this "split," but adults with borderline or narcissistic personality disorder still experience it—especially under stress.

One form this can take is to "split" the world into two rigid groups, such as winners and losers. Have you noticed how frequently Trump talks about himself, his numbers, and others in these terms? As psychologist Joseph Burgo points out in his recent book about extreme narcissists:

> Fred Trump, Donald's father, expected his sons to be ruthless competitors who showed their opponents no mercy. "Be a killer," he told them. . . . Fred Trump believed there were only two classes of people in the world – winners and losers; every Trump would of course be a winner.

GROUP SPLITTING

Why is this relevant to a book about politics? The reason is that people with this characteristic can trigger intense emotions *between other people,* such as a group of voters. Here's how one author describes the dynamic when it occurs in a treatment program for people with borderline personality disorder:

> "Staff splitting," . . . is a much-discussed phenomenon in which professionals treating borderline patients begin

arguing and fighting about a patient, the treatment plan, or the behavior of other professionals with the patient. The responsibility for the dissension among the staff is then attributed to the patient, who is said to have split the staff; hence the term "staff splitting."

HIGH-CONFLICT DISPUTES

I first learned about this dynamic in the 1980s when I was working at a psychiatric hospital. I was surprised to see it again later when I was working with legal and workplace disputes. When I train or consult with professionals who are dealing with high-conflict personalities, sometimes I have to explain this process of splitting so that they can unwind from bitterly hating each other within a work group. In addition to occurring frequently among hospital staffs, splitting happens in university departments, government agencies, business power struggles, nonprofit agencies, churches, high-profile legal disputes, and many other settings.

SPLITTING THE ELECTORATE

Unfortunately, I believe that powerful splitting is about to happen to America. Don Saposnek and I predicted these types of problems when we wrote *Splitting America,* which I quoted from at the beginning of this chapter. We already saw the signs in the last few elections. However, we did not expect such a clearly high-conflict person to run for president so soon. We believe that people will be shocked at how hostile and personal an election can become when a high-conflict candidate is involved.

Friends, family members, and neighbors will become outraged when they discover that their own friends, family members, or neighbors are for or against Donald Trump—or the next trump bubble. The intense emotions are highly contagious and pass from one person to the next, either in agreement or in opposition. This

appears to be a factor of the escalated emotions when logical thinking is shut off, a dynamic that Trump skillfully uses at his rallies
and whenever possible. There is no middle ground with splitting.
It has the following characteristics, which I have identified from
dealing with this dynamic in numerous high-conflict family and
workplace disputes:

- It's about personal qualities—like "You're stupid,
  immoral, unethical, incompetent"; "You're not a true
  American"; and other name-calling.

- It's about intense hostility—it's all emotions without
  patience or tolerance of hearing other points of view; this
  happens to both sides of a splitting argument.

- You are considered 100 percent for one side or 100
  percent for the other side—if you have ambivalence,
  someone will still hate you.

- This often leads to threats of violence or actual violence.

VIOLENCE

When splitting occurs, people feel their emotions so intensely
that it reduces their ability to restrain themselves emotionally and
verbally, which often leads to an inability to restrain themselves
physically. On March 11, 2016, many people saw the incident at
a Trump rally, where a peaceful black protester was being led out
and a white Trump follower purposefully came over and punched
him in the face, stating, "He wasn't acting like an American. . . .
The next time we see him we might have to kill him."

This loss of control tends to happen when there has already
been a large group pumping up anger toward an individual or
small group target of blame. Trump openly says threatening statements implying violence, including toward protesters at his rallies.

It's interesting that the violence on March 11 fulfilled his exact statement at an earlier event on February 23, 2016, when he himself said about a different protester, "I'd like to punch him in the face, I'll tell ya." It's the power of suggestion from a leader with intense emotions.

High-conflict leaders tend to empower their followers to adopt their preoccupation with blame (US-against-THEM thinking) and their intense and unmanaged emotions. Of course, Trump denies any responsibility for his angry rhetoric, which is standard for high-conflict leaders.

GETTING 50.1 PERCENT OF THE VOTE

The big question is whether Trump can actually get 50.1 percent of the vote needed to win the election. Of course, this is the Electoral College vote, which varies slightly from the popular vote. As of this writing, the Republican primaries are still going and Ted Cruz and John Kasich are still in the race, hoping to keep Trump short of the votes needed before the Republican Convention to clinch the party's nomination. But this book is written with the assumption that Trump is likely to be the candidate. If so, what percent of the electorate is he likely to persuade to join him in his effort to win the general election? Here's what the Pew Research Center reports about the breakdown of voters:

Based on 2014 data, 39% identify as independents, 32% as Democrats and 23% as Republicans. This is the highest percentage of independents in more than 75 years of public opinion polling.

So far, Trump has never won more than about 45 percent of the votes in his primary contests, even though he has won more than anyone else in most of these (a "plurality" of votes). I have heard radio news reports suggesting that as many as 40 percent of Republicans say they will never vote for Trump.

With these numbers, you might calculate that Trump may only attract as high as 60 percent of the 23 percent of voters who identify as Republicans—meaning about 15 percent of all voters. But there's a big wild card you may have noticed: those voters who identify as "independents." Here's a look at how they have been voting recently, as reported in the *Christian Science Monitor*:

> Voters are increasingly divided into reliably partisan camps. Those swing voters pundits love to talk about? . . . New research shows they're now about 5 percent of the US electorate—the lowest percentage ever recorded.

> . . . Fear and anger are likely causes of much of this sorting. Many voters aren't so much trying to elect their candidates as block the ones from the other party, whom they see as a danger to the republic. Negative partisanship has become one of the strongest forces in this particle physics theory of US politics.

> . . . There's evidence that [both parties] devote more attention to rallying committed supporters than reaching out to the uncommitted in presidential campaigns. They've been moving in that direction since 2000, when the virtual dead heat between George W. Bush and Al Gore showed them—and the rest of the nation—how closely balanced Republicans and Democrats are.

So if approximately half the country, including independents, actually votes Republican (and the Republican House and Senate would indicate that), we are looking at a very close race—if Trump can gain back the 40 percent of Republican who don't like him right now.

HIGH-CONFLICT MAGIC

Ironically, high-conflict disputes often end up splitting in a very similar way—almost half the group emotionally supports the high-conflict person and almost half the group says they're absurd for the following logical reasons, which they then explain with as much intensity as the emotional supporters. It almost seems like magic, how this 50-50 split occurs around so many high-conflict people whom I and others have observed. We cannot assume it will be any different with Trump, or another trump bubble candidate, just because his percentage of the electorate is so much smaller as of March 2016. It is a progressive problem with months to go as of this writing.

FAMILY POLITICS

The most frequent situation in which Don Saposnek and I have observed splitting is in high-conflict divorces, when a child becomes "alienated" against one parent and totally sides with the other. We devoted a whole chapter to this subject in our book *Splitting America.* The interesting parallel here is that the child grows to hate one parent for no logical reason. This is different from "estrangement," when there has been a history of abuse by one parent against the child.

With alienated children, their excuses for refusing all contact (with a parent with whom they used to have a loving relationship) are things like "I don't like the way he wears his hair." Or "She's no good a math and can't help me like my dad does."

The reality, after investigations and court hearings and shouting matches involving other family members, is that alienation is a bubble—it's all emotions and no realities—promoted by a parent who almost always appears to have a personality disorder (in my opinion, after about forty such cases as a lawyer or as a consultant).

Ironically, no amount of real information or admonishments from counselors, lawyers, mediators, or judges can seem to get through to an alienated child. On the contrary, such efforts often strengthen their bond with the favored parent (sometimes referred to as the "alienating parent"). The courts often give up and many children stay alienated well into adulthood. They intensely defend their favored parent the same way that Trump supporters intensely defended him after Mitt Romney gave his speech "exposing" Trump.

In other words, if the *intense-emotion-trumps-thinking* bubbles are allowed to continue in U.S. politics, this dynamic will only escalate and I believe we will sooner or later have a war on our hands. It only gets better when a larger force intervenes. High-conflict people, including high-conflict leaders, do not appear able to stop themselves.

In family courts, it's the judge who sometimes stops the high-conflict behavior. Family court judges are starting to understand the dynamics underlying alienation and requiring parents to stop exposing their intense emotions to their children and requiring reasonable contact with the "hated" parent, so that the emotional isolation with the "favored" parent doesn't lead to more endless bubbles.

With Hitler, the larger intervening force was the Allies, led by Eisenhower and U.S. troops. Germany couldn't stop itself. Instead, Hitler had acquired assistance from countries like Japan and Italy. You see, this stuff can spread if it isn't nipped in the bud. In this election, it will have to be informed voters who impact the emotionally hooked voters—especially the negative advocates.

NEGATIVE ADVOCATES

The piece that's missing in understanding how Trump could go from about 15 percent of the electorate in the primaries to 50.1 percent in the general election in November is the role of *negative advocates*, a term I coined over a decade ago to help explain the dynamics of how high-conflict people gain allies. Negative advocates are mostly well-respected, well-intentioned people who become *emotionally hooked* into supporting the all-or-nothing thinking, intense emotions, and negative behavior of a high-conflict person.

It is the intensity of the emotions that often hooks them—so they shut off their logical minds. They often catch fear without facts. But in business, in government agencies, and in work groups, it also appears that negative advocates believe—often wrongly—that the high-conflict person will help them advance their career and/or financial interests.

In Trump's case, the first high-profile negative advocate was Chris Christie, governor of New Jersey. He's a classic example of someone who was regarded as a more likeable and reasonable fellow in the Republican candidate pool, although he also had a reputation as a bully. He had some good history being flexible and moderate with President Obama, he's a fan of Bruce Springsteen (who many Democrats and Republicans love), and he had positioned himself to appeal to both moderate and conservative independents—a growing part of the electorate, as we saw above.

More members of Congress have lined up behind Trump, as have other public figures like celebrities, business owners, and sports stars. Slowly, these more moderate and likeable negative advocates will help Trump in gaining voters. And they will be passionate about it, because they are emotionally hooked *and* uninformed. They will help in blowing trump bubbles and they will succeed in many cases. And you will probably be shocked as you watch it happen.

The reality, based on my experience working with family and workplace disputes, and observing political groups, is that high-conflict people trigger two increasingly equal opposing forces: supporters who are significantly emotionally hooked (which means they're angry and ready to fight for the HCP) and opponents who are focused on the logic of the situation (and become outraged that the others don't see something so obvious and ready to fight against the HCP). I expect that we'll see this over the next several months around Trump.

ESCALATING ANGER

What seems to occur is that the angry emotions of the HCP's supporters trigger the angry emotions of the HCP's more logical opponents, which makes them both less logical and the disputes more emotional on both sides now. And as both sides become more heated, they become less reasonable and less cooperative— feeding off of each other's high-conflict emotions—and more rigid in their positions.

But then they also feel more justified in not restraining themselves and instead in expressing their anger. This group shedding of restraint becomes group hatred, which ultimately turns into violence. While it is often stoked by a high-conflict leader, the HCP is usually surprised at what has opened up. Depending on the individual's organizational leadership skills, the HCP may or may not be able to contain it and focus it for his or her purposes. Dictators are good at focusing this newly unrestrained energy. We will see if Trump has any such containment skills.

If so, we may see a successful authoritarian leader for a few months. If not, we may see significant chaos.

HOPE

At this point, you probably think I have lost my mind to paranoia or you are becoming concerned that I might be right. Perhaps you can see why I thought this little book was urgent. I can see these possibilities and hope we can turn them around before they escalate very far.

With this in mind, I want to predict that Trump will viciously attack his opponent in the general election (right now either Hillary Clinton or Bernie Sanders, more likely Hillary) in a warlike approach beyond anything we have previously seen. Remember what I have been saying: as HCPs become empowered, they don't become more reasonable—they become more aggressive. That is part of why they are HCPs, because they lack the ability for self-restraint.

However, there are principles you can use to help educate potential negative advocates, as well as bystanders who never planned to become involved and don't usually vote. Educating opponents of Trump about these patterns and principles for bursting a trump bubble should give them more energy, enthusiasm and hope for the task. Part II of this book provides several dramatic and tragic examples of trump bubbles rising and falling, as well as methods for talking with trump bubble supporters.

PART II
THE FALL

CHAPTER 7

HIGH-CONFLICT POLITICIANS AND THEIR PREDICTABLE WARS

(The Intense US-Against-THEM Pattern Ends in War)

"The impression I gained of Hitler is that of a fanatical crusader," he reported. "He has a certain forcefulness and intensity which gives him a power of leadership among those classes that do not weigh his outpourings. . . ." Many Germans were turning to the Nazis "in despair that former political allegiances provide no relief from present intolerable conditions," Sackett [the American Ambassador in 1931] acknowledged. But he predicted that "if the man comes into power he must find himself shortly on the rocks, both of international and internal difficulties. He is certainly not the type from which statesmen evolve."

—Andrew Nagorski, *Hitlerland: American Eyewitnesses to the Nazi Rise to Power*

THE FOLLOWING are a few examples of political leaders who built their bubbles on intense fear and anger, and wishful thinking and false beliefs, rather than on programs that would actually protect their followers or improve their lives.

These bubbles always seem to lead to war, because they are built on defensive emotions and the removal of self-restraints for an entire population. They escalate emotions while blocking logical information. Then they follow the leader against the leader's identified targets of blame. Here's the overall pattern I will describe in each case:

THE HCP THEORY OF HIGH-CONFLICT POLITICIANS AND WAR

The Rise (The Bubble Forms)

High-conflict personality (HCP)
+
Group resentment, fear, and anger
+
Emotional media
+
Negative advocates
=
Unrestrained aggressive behavior (war)

The Fall (The Bubble Bursts)

The HCP aggressively overreaches

Targets of blame fight back effectively

Bystanders speak up, take action

Negative advocates abandon ship

Followers turn on the HCP

HITLER'S RISE AND FALL

The HCP and His Targets of Blame

Hitler's rise was, in fact, based on a bubble. Even though there were legitimate concerns about the worsening conditions in Germany after World War I, and the Great Depression that followed it, Hitler did not have real economic solutions. He intensely focused Germans' frustrations on hatred for the Jews and dominating Europe—making Germany great again after its humiliation in World War I.

Group Resentment, Fear, and Anger

The Jews were a small minority in Germany who had gained more rights in the 1920s than they had had before. Hitler was able to focus the lower-middle class's economic resentments on this group, as though they were a powerful force taking over their lives. They were easier to see than the wealthy industrialists and bankers who had helped lead them into World War I and helped crash their economy ten years later. And they were easier to pick on.

But hatred for the Jews was a bubble that would eventually burst and accomplish nothing for Germany. It was pure *emotions without thinking*. But it did give him power for over two decades before it burst. As the ambassador said above, Hitler manipulated people who were feeling desperate and did not "weigh his outpourings." His followers just stopped thinking. Nagorski writes:

"Everybody in Germany knows that the Jews are our misfortune," one of the Nazis replied.

"But just how? Why?" Edgar [the American reporter] persisted.

"There are too many of them. And then, Jews are not people like the rest of us."

"But in my country the proportion of Jews is much higher than in Germany. But we lost no war, have not starved, not been betrayed to foreigners; in short, have suffered none of the evils you attribute to the presence of the Jews in Germany. How do you account for this?"

"We don't account for it. We simply know it is true," the Nazi replied.

Negative Advocates

Hitler did not start out with storm troopers and death camps. In fact, in his early days many justified his intense anger as representing legitimate concerns or simply viewed him as harmless. He had many *negative advocates* during his rise to power.

One of them was Ernst "Putzi" Hanfstaengl, born of an American mother and German father, who was a Harvard graduate and whose family ran art galleries in London and New York, as well as Germany where he lived. His wife was from the United States. Putzi saw Hitler speak in 1922 in Germany and was so impressed he decided that he would "educate this skillful orator who 'was clearly going to go far.'" He became Hitler's "propagandist and press advisor." However, after Hitler took power in 1933, Putzi started to have some concerns, but "nurtured the hope that he could moderate [Hitler's] excesses." Eventually, by the mid-1930s, he was pushed out by Hitler's far more aggressive propaganda chief, Joseph Goebbels.

While Putzi later claimed, after the war, that he had started to realize "how detached from reality" Hitler's entourage had become, it seems as though he wouldn't have left Germany if he hadn't been pushed out. Yet it appears it was negative advocates like Putzi who helped keep American reporters happy and lulled into believing that Hitler was not a threat—all the time that he was building up his military might and seducing the masses.

Emotional Media

Hitler was an exceptional orator and he was able to reach his followers in ever growing numbers, significantly through the rise of radio and movies. Of course, his message was one of fear and anger, combined with images of strength and future greatness. In reality, some people absorbed his intoxicating messages of greatness, while others supported him more out of fear of the Communists. This combination of fear and greatness amplified over the airwaves was apparently extremely powerful.

By 1933, because his Nazi party was getting the largest number of votes in recent parliamentary elections, he was appointed chancellor of Germany by President Hindenburg—essentially allowing him to form and run the government. The next year he convinced the parliament to grant him all its powers, so he would be able to draft the laws and implement them, "even when they might deviate from the constitution." This also gave him the ability to control the country's media and its messages.

Unrestrained Aggressive Behavior (War)
Hitler convinced the German people that he would make Germany great again, which included "taking back" land that he and many others believed rightfully belonged to the nation. But Hitler couldn't stop himself. He invaded much of Eastern Europe.

The HCP Overreaches
Hitler became too eager in his aggressive thirst for power and land. Even though he initially formed an alliance with Josef Stalin's Soviet Union/Russia, he invaded them too. Nagorski explains:

> German troops had reached the outskirts of Moscow, a direct result of Stalin's grievous miscalculations, starting with his refusal to believe that Germany would invade his country.

> But the Soviet capital was ultimately saved because Hitler committed even bigger mistakes, refusing to listen to his generals who wanted him to push directly to the Soviet capital. He ordered a diversion south to take Kiev, insisting that it was vital to seize control of the agricultural riches and raw materials of the Ukraine first. By the time

his troops resumed their drive to Moscow, they were caught in heavy autumn rains that turned Russian dirt roads into swamps, and then by swiftly plummeting temperatures. . . . [M]ost of the German troops had not even been issued winter uniforms.

Targets Fight Back
In the situation above, Hitler's overreaching gave Stalin the chance to organize troops from the eastern front to push the Germans back. This was one of the turning points in the war.

Bystanders Take Action
Finally, after the Japanese bombed Pearl Harbor in 1941, the United States declared war on Japan and Germany (and Germany declared war on the United States). In this case, three years later the American-led Allies landed at Normandy Beach in France, surprising the Germans and starting the end of World War II by taking back France and then taking over Germany. Interestingly, Hitler was unprepared and slow to respond to the Normandy invasion, not believing that he had been outwitted.

Negative Advocates Abandon Ship
Putzi Hanfstaengl was one of the negative advocates who got out safely before it was too late. Many of Hitler's negative advocates were killed off when they started to challenge him or tried to escape. Some apparently committed suicide after they realized what they had helped create and that they were doomed.

Followers Turn on the HCP
Some of Hitler's associates tried to kill him during the war, but their attempts failed—sometimes coming very close. They were immediately executed.

Conclusion
It wasn't insiders who ended Hitler's reign and burst his bubble. It was mostly the Allied troops and his own overreaching. Hitler accomplished nothing for Germany and ran his country into the

ground—as well as killed millions of innocent people, including approximately six million Jews and millions of his own soldiers. He was a pure bubble, who left his country in much more of a mess than when he started. Intense emotions trumped thinking. Imagine if the United States had not intervened and if there were no other outsiders to stop him?

JOE MCCARTHY AND HIS WAR ON COMMUNISTS IN AMERICA

High-Conflict Personality and His Targets of Blame
Joseph McCarthy was a Republican from Wisconsin who served in the U.S. Senate from 1947 to 1957. In Washington, he was a "right-wing demagogue [who] fueled a febrile atmosphere of anti-Communism, driving normally rational U. S. officials to excessive lengths to prove their devotion to the defeat of the 'Red Menace.'"

Group Resentment, Fear, and Anger
Following World War II, there was a lot of concern about the spread of communism. Russia was an established Communist country, China had gone Communist around the end of World War II, and in 1950 North Korea invaded South Korea—only to be pushed back with the help of the United States. The Cold War was in full gear and there was a concern about spies, especially from the Soviet Union. However, there was no evidence that there were people in the U.S. federal government or in Hollywood who were Communists disloyal to the United States.

Author Stanley Karnow describes McCarthy's actions: "Senator McCarthy . . . unscrupulously exploited the fall of China and the deadlocked conflict in Korea to spark an explosion of anti-Communist paranoia aimed at promoting his own influence."

Emotional Media
McCarthy was very high profile, holding televised hearings in the U.S. Senate. It was an early use of television for a political circus.

He held dramatic public hearings in which he questioned people about being Communists, who he feared would overthrow the government. People were glued to the TV, wondering who would be called next to testify against themselves—and who would fight back. It was perfect political drama.

Negative Advocates

One of McCarthy's most high-profile negative advocates was Richard Nixon, the vice president when Dwight Eisenhower was president. Karnow discusses Nixon's role:

> Nixon's crusade against the "Red menace" seemed to be motivated less by ideology than by opportunism. He derived satisfaction from nailing [Alger] Hiss because, as he divulged afterward, the case gave him "nationwide publicity." As vice-president during Eisenhower's first term, he endorsed Senator Joe McCarthy's wild witch-hunts— shifting only after McCarthy slandered Eisenhower and became a liability to the Republican party.

Another surprising negative advocate was Bobby Kennedy, the brother of future president John F. Kennedy. Apparently, their father, Joseph Kennedy, was friends with McCarthy. Author Robert Caro writes:

> In 1953, his father got him the job with McCarthy's [Senate Investigations] committee. Later his work with the committee would be glossed over, excused by saying he didn't really believe in McCarthy's anti-Communist campaign. He did. "I felt it was work that needed to be done then," he was to say. And on another occasion: "At the time, I thought there was a serious internal security threat to the United States . . . and Joe McCarthy seemed to be the only one who was doing anything about it."

Unrestrained Aggressive Behavior (War)

Over five years, McCarthy held his high-profile hearings, quizzing over 300 government officials and Hollywood types on their loyalty to the United States and demanding that they answer "Are you now or have you ever been a member of the Communist Party?"

HCP Overreaching

In 2003, 4,000 pages of transcripts from the McCarthy hearings were released. Apparently, they revealed that the senator used closed sessions to initially interview witnesses and he didn't call back for public hearings those who assertively stood up to him. If he thought they were passive enough that he could push them around, he would call them to the public hearings. Even though he threatened people with contempt of court if they didn't answer the way he wanted them to, no one ever went to jail.

His behavior was a good example of an HCP who made big headlines for five years, then became fully discredited for "McCarthyism" because of his wild and always dramatic allegations. He didn't find anyone to be a threat to the country.

Targets of Blame Fight Back

Many of those he tried to intimidate wouldn't go along with his attacks and challenged him on TV, to his great frustration.

Negative Advocates Abandon Ship

Richard Nixon shifted against McCarthy only after the Senator slandered Eisenhower and became a liability to the Republican Party.

Bobby Kennedy resigned from the committee in 1953, but apparently this was related to a dispute about his job.

Followers Turn on the HCP

Eventually, McCarthy's own political party turned against him. In 1954, the Senate censured him for his aggressive tactics with all but one Senator voting against him.

Conclusion

Joseph McCarthy's trump bubble was based on a generalized nationwide fear of Communism, which started and ended up outside the country. However, as with many trump bubbles, a fearful group will follow where the high-conflict politician leads. The country was spellbound watching the Senate hearings and hearing over and over again (like today's 24/7 news) that there was a Red Menace inside the U.S. government.

Now, the term McCarthyism is associated with any demagogue who tries to stir up people's fear against a vague target of blame with no basis. A classic trump bubble that pointlessly intimidated large sections of the country for years and helped lead to the debacle of the Vietnam War.

LYNDON JOHNSON AND THE VIETNAM WAR

High-Conflict Personality and Targets of Blame

Did Lyndon Johnson have a high-conflict personality? In the 1950s and 1960s, he had a real reputation for bullying legislators into passing the bills that he favored. After John F. Kennedy was assassinated in 1963, Johnson became president and moved several of Kennedy's initiatives through Congress. He was praised for his actions with the Civil Rights Act and the Voting Rights Act, which were major steps forward for minorities, especially African Americans. He also got Medicare through Congress, which wasn't easy but is now seen as one of the bedrock contributions of the federal government to our society and is almost universally appreciated.

The conflict in Vietnam crept up on him in his second term. In his history of the war, Karnow writes:

> Johnson especially feared that right-wing adversar-

ies would prevail over him should South Vietnam fall to Communism, just as Harry Truman [president after World War II] had been hounded by Senator Joseph McCarthy and other demagogues after the Communists engulfed China. Recollecting McCarthy's witch-hunts, he foresaw the danger of another "mean and destructive debate" that would "shatter my presidency, kill my administration and damage our democracy. If a Communist victory in Vietnam knocked over the dominoes, Johnson would be the biggest domino to topple—or so he believed.

Group Resentment, Fear, and Anger

The big fear in those days, as in the 1950s, was Communists. The "Domino Theory" became popular, based on the idea that North Vietnam had gone Communist and that South Vietnam would soon—and then the next thing you know, they'll be landing on our shores. We were in a missile race with the Communist Soviet Union and Communist China couldn't be trusted, although it was much poorer. The targets of blame that needed to be bombed into submission were poor Vietnamese farmers, but the big picture scared a lot of people.

By the 1960s, the atmosphere still held a lot of fear of Communists, especially because the Soviet Union and the United States had numerous nuclear missiles pointed at each other.

But at first we only had advisers in Vietnam. Why did it escalate?

In 1964 there were two incidents two days apart, on August 2 and August 4, in which it seemed that North Vietnamese boats had fired on a U.S. boat patrolling in international waters or possibly North Vietnamese waters, depending on which boundaries at sea were being followed—a vague situation indeed. This triggered open warfare. But here is how history describes it, in the words of Karnow:

Subsequent research by both official and unofficial investigators has indicated with almost total certainty that the second Communist attack never happened. It had not been deliberately faked, but Johnson and his staff, desperately seeking a pretext to act vigorously, had seized upon a fuzzy set of circumstances to fulfill a contingency plan. Much of the truth was to trickle out in the years ahead. . . .

McNamara [Secretary of Defense] was probably sincere when he told Admiral Sharp that reprisals against the Communists could not be carried out until "we are damned sure" of what happened. However, Johnson ordered the retaliatory air strikes against North Vietnam despite a lack of hard evidence, leaving McNamara with the job of justifying the action.

Losing no time, on August 5, Johnson used this incident to seek a resolution that would authorize him to "take all necessary measures" to repel attacks against U.S. forces and to "prevent further aggression." This became known as the Gulf of Tonkin Resolution.

The true information about the United States' entry into the Vietnam War under false pretenses was suppressed for decades. Likewise, the true information about how the war was going was suppressed. Yet Johnson pressed forward in escalating the war, which was primarily being fought by young men who were drafted into the Army.

Emotional Media

The news media also seemed to enthusiastically support the war effort. Karnow writes, "Opinion polls showed that 85 percent of the American public stood behind the administration, and most newspaper editorials faithfully reflected this support."

Walter Cronkite, the news anchorman for CBS during the 1960s, calmly appeared to support and report the news about the

Vietnam War. The nation often watched the evening news together.

Negative Advocates

There were many negative advocates supporting the war in both the Republican and the Democratic Parties. But perhaps one of the key negative advocates for Johnson in this war was Robert Mc-Namara, Secretary of Defense under both Kennedy and Johnson. He was extremely smart, knew his numbers, and seemed to know exactly what he was doing. He had easily served as a negative advocate for Johnson for escalating the war with the Gulf of Tonkin Resolution. Karnow writes:

> He now mobilized two men to promote the document. One was McNamara, who could dazzle legislators with his maps and flip-charts. The other was Fulbright, chairman of the Senate Foreign Relations Committee.
>
> On August 5, though the Tonkin Gulf puzzle had not yet been pieced together, Johnson sent his resolution to Congress for approval. A day later, McNamara appeared before a joint session of the Senate foreign relations and armed services committees to persuade their members to endorse the resolution rapidly. It was plain from the beginning that he would face little opposition.

Soon, McNamara was running the war and most advisers and citizens trusted the wisdom of this brilliant war technician.

Unrestrained Aggressive Behavior (War)

Starting in March 1965, after he had been re-elected, Johnson sent combat troops to Vietnam for the first time. He eventually had an army of 500,000 U.S. soldiers in Vietnam.

The HCP Overreaches

But Johnson overreached when it came to Vietnam. Even though the U.S. involvement had started before he became president, he is the one most responsible for its escalation into a major war that killed over 50,000 U.S. soldiers and triggered some of the most intense protests in the United States of the twentieth century.

The Vietnam War escalated between 1964 and 1968, despite all the protests and despite what Johnson knew about the reality that the United States was losing the war. He kept it going and escalated it up to 500,000 soldiers at its peak. He couldn't be the one to look weak in the face of the enemy.

The Vietnam War brought out intense anger within the United States fairly quickly. Student protesters started out as very small groups and the reaction to them was intense. Soon street protestors and military supporters ended up in pushing and shoving matches, which sometimes turned violent. Within a few years, everyone seemed angry and some were violent. There was a huge split in the country.

Half the country was emotionally attached to the war, primarily out of fear of Communism but also out of fear of protesters and a sense of chaos taking over the nation. The other half of the country questioned the logic of the war and became increasingly angry at having young people sent over there to die for no reason.

Targets Fight Back

Despite being poor farmers, the Viet Cong (supported by North Vietnam) were beating the U.S.-supported South Vietnamese troops. Despite escalations against them, they were winning the war. They slowly chased the Americans and their South Vietnamese army top commanders out of the country—although that didn't finish until 1975, years after Johnson left office.

Bystanders Speak Up

At this time in history, protesters were starting to have an impact on government officials. A few U.S. senators and representatives grew to support the student protesters, as well as union members, civil rights activists, and university faculty and administrators.

Negative Advocates Abandon Ship

People with great credibility who had once supported the war started to question it publicly. One of the turning points occurred when Walter Cronkite expressed his doubt about the war during his TV nightly news broadcast. This was when Johnson apparently said, "If I've lost Cronkite, I've lost the nation." This is how it seems to go when negative advocates remove their support of an HCP's bubble.

Followers Turn on the HCP

By the time the next presidential election was getting geared up in 1968, Johnson realized that he had lost the support of the country he would need to win re-election. Rather than face that humiliation, he decided not to run. His bubble had burst and it was time to go.

Conclusion

Of course, this is a superficial treatment of Johnson and the Vietnam War. But the result was a tragedy for the 50,000 U.S. soldiers who lost their lives there, all the soldiers who returned to an unwelcoming country, and millions of Vietnamese killed and dispossessed. The United States gained no benefit from it and fifty years later it's clear that they were not a threat to us. It was a bubble driven by fear of Communists coming to our borders under the Domino Theory. Even then, there was no logic in it. But a high-conflict politician, his negative advocates, and the media couldn't resist the urge to go to war.

Johnson also, for all of his experience and self-confidence, did not understand who he was dealing with in Southeast Asia. Karnow summarizes:

> That primitive bluster also masked Johnson's discomfort in the complicated realm of international affairs. The strange names, places and customs puzzled him. During

a visit as vice president to Bangkok, he flew into a rage when a staff member of the American embassy counseled him against shaking hands with the Thais, who traditionally recoil from physical contact with strangers. Dammit, Johnson exploded, he shook hands with people everywhere, and they loved it. Nor could he comprehend his inability to bargain with foreign leaders the way he haggled with American politicians, businessmen and labor negotiators. In 1965, to cite an example, he was baffled by Ho Chi Minh's [president of North Vietnam] rejection of his offer of a huge economic project to develop the Mekong valley in exchange for concessions to end the Vietnam war. "Old Ho can't turn me down, old Ho can't turn me down," he repeated after making the offer. In his mind, Ho was no different from George Meany, the labor leader, with whom he regularly struck such deals.

Reading this reminds one easily of Donald Trump, the ever-confident negotiator and deal-maker. If Lyndon Johnson, a very experienced lifetime politician, had difficulty making deals with such different cultures, just imagine the Donald offending and misreading the leaders he would have to deal with as president. If Johnson "flew into a rage" about not being able to shake hands, imagine what Trump would fly into a rage about.

CHAPTER 8

THE IRAQ WAR BUBBLE AND BEYOND

*(Yesterday's US-Against-THEM
Creates Today's US-Against-THEM)*

"The [order] formally disbanded the Iraqi army, which had largely disappeared on its own. In some ways, the orders achieved their objectives. Iraq's Shia and Kurds—the majority of the population—welcomed the clean break from Saddam. But the orders had a psychological impact I did not foresee. Many Sunnis took them as a signal they would have no place in Iraq's future. This was especially dangerous in the case of the army. Thousands of armed men had just been told they were not wanted. Instead of signing up for the new military, many joined the insurgency."
— George W. Bush, *Decision Points*

GEORGE W. BUSH AND THE WAR IN IRAQ

High-Conflict Personality and Targets of Blame

When George W. Bush heard about the attacks on September 11, 2001, the first words he apparently spoke when he got on Air Force One were "Heads are going to roll!" He didn't say: "What did we miss?" "What should we do now?" This fits with his reputation for never self-reflecting and also saying "I don't do nuance." He appeared to be preoccupied with blaming others. This, and his negative advocates, may have gotten him into the Iraq War—totally unrelated to the 9/11 attacks, but one of his targets of blame.

Group Resentment, Fear, and Anger

For a couple days, the world showed an outpouring of sympathy for the United States and the families of the victims—even Palestinians held a candlelight vigil. This could have been an opportunity to unite the world against the tiny band of thugs who carried out this criminal act. But instead, Bush adopted an all-or-nothing approach, picking the largest possible targets of blame: Islamic fundamentalists around the world.

It didn't take long for the country's resentment to turn into anger and hatred for Muslims. Since they are only 1 percent of the U.S. population, they were a good example of the "other" that the people could easily hate. Since they were far away, they took on a larger evil status. But then Muslims who were in the United States experienced threats and some incidents of violence. The pure emotions of fear and anger against a minority group can be hard to restrain once a leader seems to endorse them.

But Bush soon focused the nation's fear and anger on Saddam Hussein and Iraq in a bubble of unrelated, pumped-up warfare based on a false report that Hussein was looking for material to make nuclear weapons. Bush created the next US-against-THEM war based on a bubble of finding "weapons of mass destruction" (WMD).

Emotional Media

The media seemed to love the war in Iraq. Correspondents were embedded within the troops. And with the advent of cable news channels, it was Iraq War 24/7. American flags sprouted up everywhere and many citizens even stopped eating French fries when France refused to join us in this war. The media was so dramatic and persuasive that when Bush ran for re-election in 2004, over 70 percent of his likely voters believed that our troops had found WMD after invading Iraq—even though Bush himself admitted that they hadn't. The power of repetition for all those months before the war was embedded in people's memories!

Negative Advocates

In order to gain international support for invading Iraq, Bush had Colin Powell give a speech at the United Nations. Powell was a four-star general, former chairman of the Joint Chiefs of Staff, and the current secretary of state. He was popular with both the Democratic and Republican Parties. He reluctantly agreed to make the case in favor of military action against Hussein. He claimed that Hussein had biological weapons and was working to obtain material to make nuclear weapons.

Upon hearing from this highly credible military man—who possessed much more credibility than George W. Bush—many Democratic Senators, including Senators Hillary Clinton and Dianne Feinstein, voted to authorize Bush to go to war against Hussein if he himself deemed it necessary.

Unfortunately, it turned out that the information Powell presented was based on false reports and there were no WMD nor was Hussein trying to obtain nuclear material. This is a classic example of a negative advocate for a high-conflict politician helping promote a bubble as the basis for a war. All emotion and no substance.

Unrestrained Aggressive Behavior (War)

Of course, Bush didn't like nuance so he went to war. He could have kept trying diplomacy, like his father often did and Colin Powell had strongly encouraged, but he seemed attracted to the certainty of an invasion.

He also had another negative advocate in his secretary of defense, Donald H. Rumsfeld. Rumsfeld spoke like Donald Trump—in exaggerated terms of reassurance. He spoke of the Iraqi people greeting the American ("Coalition") forces with open arms and flowers. He said that Hussein's troops would quickly give in to the "shock and awe" of the trimmed down military force we were sending. He used dramatic language that would have made Donald Trump proud. A bubble of confidence without substance.

HCP Overreaches

In this war, part of the overreaching was not having a large enough ground force for the job. This was primarily Rumsfeld's doing, as he was so overconfident that the Iraqis would love us. Likewise, he was caught off guard by the improvised explosive devices (IEDs) that the insurgents would use against our troops.

Another grand overreach by Bush was removing too much of the Baath political party and military command structure that Hussein had developed, described in Bush's statement at the beginning of this chapter.

Targets of Blame Fight Back

IEDs became the way that the insurgents fought back against the "coalition" forces (essentially, the U.S. forces). No one predicted how effective these would be at killing or maiming soldiers and dragging on the war. Just as in Vietnam, local people apparently can be extremely effective at resisting much larger and sophisticated armies.

In addition, by pushing too many people out of the governmental power structure in Iraq, Bush created the forces that would attack Americans for years to come and that eventually made up the military brains of ISIS. There has been no victory in Iraq—a bubble of "shock and awe" without substance.

Bystanders Speak Up

In the 2008 presidential election, the Iraq War—and Barack Obama's opposition to it from the start—were big factors in Obama's victory. The electorate was tired of the war and Obama promised to wind it down.

Negative Advocates Abandon Ship

Colin Powell got out of the Bush administration early, in 2005, as it became clear that his caution was no longer wanted. He constantly clashed with Rumsfeld, who was in charge of the war even though Powell was supposed to be in charge of the political reconstruction of the country and foreign policy in the Middle East. Powell's stellar reputation had been tarnished by his role as a major negative advocate in the eyes of Congress and the people of the United States.

Followers Turn on HCP

The destabilization and chaos that has occurred in Iraq and the Middle East since the invasion in 2003 has convinced a majority of Americans that the War in Iraq was a mistake. Ironically, Donald Trump used this reality against George W. Bush's brother Jeb in candidate debates in early 2016. During most of his candidacy, Jeb Bush kept his brother out of sight. George W. Bush has been mostly out of the public eye since the end of his second term, when he left office with one of the lowest approval ratings of a president. His bubble burst.

Conclusion

George W. Bush was not an obvious high-conflict person, but after September 11 his approach included a preoccupation with blaming others (as president, he said he didn't self-reflect and didn't regret things he did), all-or-nothing thinking (going to war before diplomacy had been exhausted), intense emotions (reflected primarily in his references to fighting an Axis of Evil and the frequent use of the term "evil"), and extreme behavior (invading another sovereign nation).

His rhetoric since 9/11 has inflamed the radical Muslim world and stirred up much more chaos than existed before his invasion of Iraq. Several countries have become destabilized. By transferring a bubble of fear and anger from the perpetrators of the 9/11 attacks to Iraq and Saddam Hussein, he left our country in a much more vulnerable, unstable, and internally conflicted condition. He rose in popularity with an approximately 80 percent approval rating after his response to 9/11, then fell in disgrace to a rating around 20 percent by the time he left office.

SARAH PALIN AND THE WAR ON THE ESTABLISHMENT

High-Conflict Personality and Targets of Blame

In August 2008, the Republicans were trying to distance themselves from George W. Bush and selected the popular "maverick" politician John McCain as their presidential candidate. After Barack Obama's stirring acceptance speech to nearly 100,000 people at the end of the Democratic convention, he and his vice presidential candidate, Joe Biden, were riding high.

Five days later, the Republicans would have their convention. Then, McCain pulled the biggest coup of all. He announced his vice presidential nominee and took the country by storm—and most of the momentum away from Barack Obama. Her name was Sarah Palin. Authors John Heilemann and Mark Halperin describe Palin:

> She was forty-four years old, had occupied the Alaska statehouse for twenty months, and had an 80 percent approval rating, making her, as Schmidt point out, "the most popular governor in America." She'd attended five colleges

and been a beauty queen, a sportscaster, and the two-term mayor of Wasilla, the tiny town where she lived with her snowmobiling husband, Todd, and five children. She was pro-life, anti-stem cell research, pro-gun, and pro-states rights. She had captured the governorship by running as a reformer, pledging to clean up the corrupt clubhouse politics of Juneau, and she was often at odds with Alaska's regnant Republican kingpin, Senator Ted Stevens. Her nickname from her high school basketball days was "Sarah Barracuda." She was intensely competitive, apparently fearless, and endlessly watchable.

She had the potential for a high-conflict personality, with a nickname Sarah Barracuda, but her targets of blame were not yet obvious. John McCain, in an effort to grab the momentum, had quickly named someone who was not obvious even to him. High-conflict politicians often start out with a sugarcoating. But she was getting ready to show her true colors. As Palin is quoted by Heilemann and Halperin:

> "You know what they say the difference between a hockey mom and a pit bull is?" she said. "Lipstick!"

Group Resentment, Fear, and Anger—and Love

Palin immediately found an enthusiastic audience for her energetic and upbeat style. She had an automatic audience with all Republicans—who had been feeling hopeless after the George W. Bush debacle and the excitement around Barack Obama—but she especially energized Republican women. The economy was falling apart, with companies starting to go out of business with the housing and stock market bubbles collapsing around them in September and October 2008. But the full effects of that had not yet sunken in. Palin's positive energy swept the Republican Party off its feet. Heilemann and Halperin write:

Donations and volunteers spiked up. Cable and radio could talk of little else but Sarah. The Palin pick deprived Obama of his post-convention bump; the weekend after the GOP convention, McCain was trailing him by a trifling two points. And according to an ABC News/ *Washington Post* poll, McCain's standing among white women had improved by a net twenty points (from 50-42 behind Obama to 53-41 ahead) in the blink of an eye.

Emotional Media

Palin was a gift to Fox News. Gabriel Sherman recounts:

> Ailes, watching the Republican convention, was riveted by the appearance of an exotic political creature: Sarah Palin. "She hit a home run," he told executives the next day. Her gleeful establishment bashing made her a perfect heroine for a new Ailes story line—and Fox's ratings soared to a cable news record. During Palin's speech, Fox attracted more than nine million viewers, eclipsing every other news network, cable or broadcast.

While she quickly demonstrated little ability for critical thinking and almost no knowledge of national and world affairs, her emotional appeal was incredible and made to order for emotional media. Her emotional appeal without thinking gave her all the makings of a trump bubble, but few people realized it at that time. Sherman writes:

> Partly because of her embarrassing campaign interview with Katie Couric, and partly because of her outlandish family life and moose-shooting habits, Palin was a massive American celebrity. . . .
>
> Weeks after [they lost] the 2008 election, reality show producer Mark Burnett, the creator of *Survivor*, called Palin and pitched her on starring in her own show. . . .

Palin made it clear to Fox that she wouldn't be willing to move to New York or Washington. Fox offered to build a remote camera hookup in her Wasilla home. . . . In January 2010, Palin finally had her $1 million-a-year deal.

Negative Advocates

In Palin's case, her biggest negative advocate was Roger Ailes, head of Fox News. It was a mutually productive relationship. She was part of his team of potential presidential candidates—yes, there was talk in 2009, 2010, and 2011 of her running—and his plan to counter the Obama administration in every way he could. Sherman writes:

> Hiring Palin brought the number of prospective presidential candidates on Ailes's payroll to five. . . . Presidential politics were what brought viewers, and in the Obama age, Ailes was dominating both politics and business. Fox was on track to generate nearly a billion-dollar profit. . . . The Obama era turnaround plan was firing on all cylinders. Ailes "predicted that the Democrats would lose the House," one senior producer said. Ailes was right. In the midterms, Republicans would retake the House in the biggest electoral gain since 1948.

Unrestrained Aggressive Behavior (War)

Sarah Palin had helped Ailes win his war against the Democrats (at least in Congress) and he had helped her launch a media career with her war on the establishment. In fact, she was one of the original high-profile politicians to support Tea Party candidates against the mainstream Republican candidates in the 2010 House election—and many of them won. She was a high-profile leader on Fox News and in the Republican Party. At times it seemed as though it was all-Sarah all-the-time on the news, including the mainstream news.

HCP Overreaches

As part of her war rhetoric, Palin put images of rifle target cross-hairs on her website, naming specific congressional candidates who were "targeted" for defeat in November 2010. Unfortunately, a disturbed young man absorbed that message too well and went to a shopping mall gathering one morning in January 2011, where Democratic representative Gabrielle ("Gabby") Giffords was meeting with constituents. He shot her in the head and killed six other people. Giffords survived, but was seriously injured.

Targets of Blame and Bystanders Fight Back

Palin was soundly criticized in the press for encouraging violence with the images and rhetoric on her website. She quickly took them down. However, the damage was done.

Negative Advocates Abandon Ship

Roger Ailes was already concerned, even before this event. Sherman describes what happened next:

> Ailes began to doubt Palin's political instincts. He thought she was getting bad advice from her kitchen cabinet and saw her erratic behavior as a sign that she was a "loose cannon." A turning point in their relationship came in the midst of the national debate over the Tucson shooting massacre, which left congresswoman Gabrielle Giffords almost fatally wounded. As the media pounced on Palin's violent rhetoric—her website had put the image of a target on Giffords's congressional district months earlier to mobilize her voters to defeat Giffords at the polls—Palin wanted to fight back, angry that commentators were singling her out. Ailes agreed but told her to stay out of it. He thought if she stayed quiet, she would score a victory.

"Lie low," he told her. "If you want to respond later, fine, but do not interfere with the memorial service."

Palin ignored Ailes's advice and went ahead and released her controversial "blood libel" video the morning Obama traveled to Tucson. For Ailes, her decision was further evidence that she was flailing around off-message. . . . "He thinks Palin is an idiot," a Republican close to Ailes said. . . . What had been an effort to boost ratings became a complication. . . .

"Why are you letting Palin have the profile?" Karl Rove said to Ailes in one meeting. "Why are you letting her go on your network and say the things she's saying? . . . These are alternative people who will never be elected, and they'll kill us."

Followers Turn on HCP

Palin's incredible ratings were slowly dropping off. In the spring in 2011, she announced that she would not run for president. Even though Fox kept her on the payroll as a commentator, her trump bubble had burst—for all the world to see that she was not a thinker and would never be president.

Conclusion

Sarah Palin's trump bubble skyrocketed faster than any of the other bubbles described in this book, after being catapulted into the presidential race of 2008. But within three years, she washed out. While she's still around, she flamed out as the public became aware of her lack of knowledge and lack of thinking. Like Donald Trump, she gave the impression of knowledge because of her confidence. But confidence says nothing about substance.

While she didn't start a world war, her war against the establishment ended up costing several people their lives when Gabby Giffords was shot—very likely because of Palin's escalated rhetoric and website about shooting down her identified targets of blame. Just as Trump likes to think that his rhetoric does not influence people to punch protesters in the face, Palin denied all responsibility for her over-the-top way of blaming others.

Ironically, she resurfaced to endorse and introduce Donald Trump at a rally in 2016. Her patterns of speech were extremely emotional and her knowledge does not appear to have grown. Her personality pattern has not changed at all. She demonstrates, as so many other high-conflict politicians do, that what you see is what you are always going to get.

Summary

These examples in the last two chapters demonstrate the pattern of the rise and fall of high-conflict politicians. Two led our country into huge wars that were bubbles—based on emotions of fear, anger, and love, without substance. Both the Vietnam War and the Iraq War were based on significantly false information. Our country is worse off for its involvement in both of these bubble wars, as well as for the diversions of McCarthyism and Palin war-talk.

Today's problem of terrorism and ISIS can be directly related to the destabilizing effect of the Iraq War bubble. This is one of the few accurate observations that Donald Trump has made. However, his own impulsive and contradictory statements about dealing with the Middle East suggest that he would easily make the same types of mistakes himself.

This is in stark contrast to other U.S. presidents who have dealt with international confrontations. For example, the way that President John F. Kennedy dealt with the Cuban Missile Crisis demonstrated significant restraint that made all the difference in getting the Soviet Union to remove their missiles from Cuba without a shot being fired.

Likewise, the unified force that President George H.W. Bush led to reverse Saddam Hussein's invasion of Kuwait in the Gulf

War showed remarkable restraint—and no overreaching. We got in and we got out. These are the actions of presidents who do not appear to have had high-conflict personalities. Karnow writes:

> In January 1991, when President George [H.W.] Bush unleashed a U.S. offensive against Iraq following its occupation of Kuwait, he did so only after mobilizing United Nations support in an effort to dramatize that America was not acting alone. Announcing the attack, moreover, he sought to exorcise the specter of Southeast Asia by pledging that "this will not be another Vietnam."

With this history in mind, it is imperative that we don't elect someone for president who appears to have a high-conflict personality and who also appears to have the same oratorical skills and obsessive drive to prove that he is superior to everyone else that Hitler had. The danger of starting a new trump bubble war is too high.

. . . .

CHAPTER 9

HOW TO TALK TO TRUMP BUBBLE SUPPORTERS

(Respectfully, without Anger, Arrogance, or Sarcasm)

"Morality binds and blinds. It binds us into ideological teams that fight each other as though the fate of the world depended on our side winning each battle. It blinds us to the fact that each team is composed of good people who have something important to say."

—Jonathan Haidt, *The Righteous Mind: Why Good People Are Divided by Politics and Religion*

I N THIS CHAPTER, I suggest how to talk to Trump followers and to his potential negative advocates, who aren't followers yet but might become followers over the next several months. I encourage you to also tell your friends who are opposed to Trump about these principles, so that they don't feed the anger of both sides. We all need to calm down so we can think clearly. And if Trump is no longer a candidate, these principles may apply to whatever surprising new actions he takes, or those of the next trump bubble.

USE EAR STATEMENTS

In high-conflict disputes, people often become stuck in their defensive, protective right brains and have difficulty thinking rationally in their left brains. Remember, intense emotions shut off logical thinking. For most of the past decade, our High Conflict Institute trainers have been teaching family members, employees, managers, government officials, and others to use "EAR statements" when dealing with high-conflict situations. These statements— which show empathy, attention, and/or respect— help people calm down and consider new information.

Empathy: These statements tell the listener that you have empathy for or can identify with their concerns, their situation, their feelings of frustration, and other aspects of their experience. "I can see your frustration with the way things have been going."

Attention: These statements let the person know that you will listen, that you are interested, that you want to know more about their perspective. "Tell me more. I want to understand your point of view."

Respect: When using these statements, you might say that you respect the person's thoughtfulness about an issue, or their efforts to solve a problem, or their skills in managing a task or project. "I have a lot of respect for how hard you have worked on your house, your job, your committee, your community, your family, etc."

EAR statements calm people's upset emotions, making it much more possible to think, ask questions, and consider other viewpoints without having to get defensive. Your statements can include any one of these—empathy, attention, or respect—or all three. They calm the emotional relationship brain (generally the right hemisphere) and make it possible to consider conflicting information and new ideas (generally the left side of the brain). They help people connect with each other with a positive attitude.

Example of Talking to a Trump Follower

The media emphasizes polarization, as it grabs people's attention so that they can gain market share of viewers in a competitive media environment. But in reality, people are not as polarized as you might think. What you see on TV is the exception, not the rule. Therefore, you don't have to assume that you are adversaries with Trump followers. I'll give an example of using EAR statements with a Trump follower.

I travel a lot giving seminars and recently I was getting a ride to a hotel with a Trump supporter, although I didn't know it at the start. Our conversation focused on chitchat, and then something was said about politics:

"What do you think of Donald Trump?" I asked.

"Oh, I agree with him. I'm voting for him."

"What do you like about him?" I inquired.

"He's strong. He tells it like it is. He's not under anyone else's control. He doesn't owe anyone anything. He'll shake up Washington. He'll investigate the Federal Reserve and other agencies that are screwing us. He'll stop sending jobs overseas. The economy's pretty messed up. It's so hard to get a good job these days." This man appeared to be in his early thirties, white, self-assured—and driving a hotel shuttle.

"Yeah, I know what you mean," I replied. "It was so much easier when I was starting out to get a job. There were a lot of interesting, good jobs, and you didn't need any training. The economy was much more fair then."

"What do *you* think of Trump?" he asked.

"He worries me. I was reading a book about Hitler over the holidays and they have a lot of similarities."

"That's crazy," he said. "People shouldn't compare him to Hitler. He's totally different."

"Well, let me read you something from the book," I said as I pulled out my iPhone and tapped on an old email with an article I had written quoting from the book, titled *Hitlerland*. I read it out loud:

> There were those who met Hitler [in the 1920's] and recognized he represented almost a primeval force and possessed an uncanny ability to tap into the emotions and anger of the German people, and those who dismissed him as a clownish figure who would vanish from the political scene as quickly as he had appeared.

"That's like what they're saying about Trump. That's interesting," he replied.

"Do you want to hear something else?" I asked.

"Okay."

I read the following, also from the book *Hitlerland*, about an observer at a speech Hitler gave at a meeting hall in 1922:

> As Hitler talked about everyday life, I observed a young woman who could not tear her eyes away from the speaker. Transfixed as if in some devotional ecstasy, she had ceased to be herself and was completely under the spell of Hitler's despotic faith in Germany's future greatness.

"So Hitler was saying he wanted to make Germany great again," I said. "Just like Trump's hats. That scares me."

He was surprised: "Hitler really said that?"

"Essentially he did. And that was when he was just getting started in the 1920s. The actions he took to make Germany great again led them right into World War II."

"Huh," the driver said. He seemed quiet and reflective for a few moments.

Then we went on to other subjects and never discussed Trump or Hitler again. But I think I got him thinking. To me, that is the goal. When Trump's followers start thinking about other perspectives, his seductive bubble of total emotion may burst.

In this conversation, I tried to offer empathy and respect for the job dilemmas of being in his early thirties in 2016. But most important, I just asked what he thought and I listened without interrupting him and without directly criticizing Trump.

2. AVOID DIRECTLY CRITICIZING TRUMP

The essence, I believe, is to not increase defensiveness. If you get angry, criticize Trump intensely, or use sarcasm or arrogance, I believe you will strengthen the person's bond to Trump.

Remember the research I mentioned early in chapter 2? Because of our human trait of *groupishness*, when group members receive more accurate information from outside the group, it tends to reinforce their commitment to the loved leader and to the group rather than to pull them away.

That's what happened when Mitt Romney said Trump was "a phony, a fraud" and a "con artist." Trump has already immunized his followers against such talk. Trump uses Twitter and his rallies to shut off people's logical thinking and to be critical of the press. His followers get defensive on his behalf. All they hear is that you are attacking the leader who speaks up for them and cares about them.

3. BE SINCERE

Tone of voice gives away a lot. When I heard Mitt Romney give his statement about Trump, he sounded slightly arrogant, slightly sarcastic, and slightly superior. These are extremely bad ways to present such serious information. Romney just sounded like another candidate giving a speech criticizing an opponent in an election.

You need to *be* sincere and *sound* sincere. After all, this is serious. These are the types of qualities that calm the right brain so that people will listen to you. Even slight insincerity triggers greater defensiveness for people already feeling disregarded and defensive in the political world.

4. AVOID LABELS

Labeling anyone anything slightly negative can trigger unnecessary defensiveness and polarization. Calling Trump "a phony, a fraud" and a "con artist" builds instant resistance for those who support him. It's totally unnecessary. Instead, provide factual information, such as I did with the hotel driver.

5. GIVE BIFF RESPONSES IN WRITING

Another one of our most popular methods for dealing with high-conflict situations is to use BIFF Responses in writing. BIFF stands for brief, informative, friendly, and firm. Generally, these statements are used when responding to a hostile email or Facebook post, but they can be used in any situation and even when talking in person. Here's an example if you were responding to an angry email from a Trump follower, such as this:

> How dare you imply that I'm an idiot for liking Trump! You're the idiot for not realizing how he is going to save the country from chaos. I mean, look at those protesters. Don't they have any respect for freedom of speech? They're the real Nazis who want to take over the world. I mean, look at how politically correct they want US to be. I'm happy when Trump says stuff that pisses them off. You should be too! They deserve a punch in the face!!
>
> Joe

Here's a BIFF Response to that:

Hi Joe,

Thanks for letting me know what you're thinking. Trump worries me when he talks about punching people. I value our friendship and don't want to let politics get in the way.

You take care,

Bill

In reality, just treating your friend respectfully will go further than arguing with him about Trump. You've said you're concerned and that's all you need to say on the subject. Valuing Joe's friendship is more important and he will appreciate that—and maybe reconsider what you have to say.

6. PRACTICE SELF-RESTRAINT

The overall message here is that there's no benefit in having a heated argument with friends, family, and strangers about politics. Heated arguments rarely persuade people. Logical reasoning has a better chance, if presented without negative emotions and insults. So practice restraining yourself from insulting, yelling at, or otherwise confronting Trump followers with anger or arrogance.

If you can remember to practice these tips, then you can go on to explain the predictable patterns of high-conflict politicians.

7. EXPLAIN THE TRUMP BUBBLE PATTERNS

Personalities have patterns—we all do. But high-conflict personalities have narrower patterns of behavior that they repeat and repeat in many different settings. This makes them more predictable and observable—well before their fall begins. As with all relationships, if you know the warning signs to look for, you can tell who to avoid and who deserves your commitment.

In the prior two chapters, I talked about patterns of high-conflict bubbles that had already risen and fallen. Now I want to point out some of the warning signs of high-conflict patterns that Trump has displayed and ways to talk about them with Trump supporters and potential negative advocates who may become enamored with Trump.

In a sense, this is like the few people who saw the mortgage bubble before it burst in 2008. Only a few people saw the pattern in advance and made huge amounts of money from this knowledge before the bubble burst.

My goal is to teach people some of the warning signs about the future, based on Trump's present behavior, so that his bubble doesn't rise much further and take us all down when it falls.

Emotional Patterns of Speech

In a primary debate in February 2016, New Jersey governor Chris Christie told the audience that senator Marco Rubio had a noticeable speech pattern: He continually repeated his same talking points as the answer to a variety of questions. And then, almost immediately, Rubio did it again! He fulfilled his own exposure. This was a severely damaging moment to his campaign and perhaps the beginning of the end. It was one of the first times I saw a politician showing awareness of speech patterns and using this knowledge as a weapon.

The following patterns of speech of Donald Trump are noticeable and familiar to me as belonging with certain types of high-conflict people. They may be subtle if you don't know to look for them. But if you explain these to people, then they can't help but notice them as they listen to him in the future. The goal here is to become aware of how much Trump's speech patterns distract listeners from useful information in evaluating a candidate.

Speed

One of the first things I noticed about Donald Trump's speech was that his words flow quickly, unlike the careful statements of many other politicians and candidates. Trump gets out many times as many words compared to the other candidates. This is similar to fast talkers in court or in the workplace, who are often high-conflict people. He exudes a confidence that the others don't quite have, which can be quite powerful in persuading people to join him. People who speak this way can slide a lot of words under the radar without giving anyone time to think about or evaluate the words they have heard.

Deception

This is one reason that people don't challenge him—they don't absorb what he says logically, but they absorb his *tone of voice*, which they find quite appealing. This is a characteristic I have seen with certain types of high-conflict personalities who practice a lot of deception, especially in relationships. It doesn't surprise me that fact-checking journalists have found over 70 percent of Trump's fact statements to be false. But his followers don't care—they already know that they love him. Talking about facts is talking to the "wrong" brain (the left brain—see chapter 1).

Seductive

Not only is he fast with his words, but he is also seductive. He is having a relationship with his followers that few politicians attempt to have. His speech moves from aggressive to intimate and back again. This is very powerful glue in relationships—this combination of strength and intimacy, especially for male speakers in attracting females. He is seducing his audiences with his words and body language. He is very effective at confidently switching back and forth from aggressive to friendly to intimate to humorous to aggressive again. He exudes confidence in these abilities, which keep everyone else off balance.

Implied Intimacy

There is the implied intimacy of a close relationship in Trump's tone of voice, even when he talks to news reporters in one-to-one interviews—even when he's being interviewed over the phone. He acts and sounds like he and the interviewer are very close buddies. There's a relaxed "you know me" quality to these conversations that neutralizes the interviewer's ability to challenge him, because it feels like they are really close buddies and close buddies don't embarrass each other in public. You almost don't want to upset him, because we're having such a close buddy moment.

Flexible Face

Trump has a very expressive and flexible face. Remember the power of face and voice news? The more variety and extreme facial movements, the more compelling and powerful an effect one can have on viewers. Trump's face has exaggerated expressions: Anger with his mouth wide open as he's speaking, like a gorilla in an aggressive stance threatening dominance. Humorous impatience with a smug mouth, as though he is barely tolerating what others are saying, but is just chuckling to himself. His smiles are big and gregarious—but they don't last, as his face is constantly in motion, whether he is speaking or not.

Bottom Line

His voice and face demand attention and respect. And if you give him those, he will reward you with implied intimacy—but just for a moment. You might say that all politicians do this, and you might be right to an extent. But Trump really does this bigger and better. That is why he is potentially dangerous. This is under most people's radar, so they give him their power without even realizing it and knowing what he will do with it.

His Own Words

Perhaps one of the most effective methods of exposing and deflating a trump bubble is to use the person's own words. The best example of this with Donald Trump is his disparaging remarks against women. Just educating people about the actual statements he has made can have a powerful effect, even on Trump's supporters, which this recent television ad has tried to do:

> "Look at that face. Would anyone vote for that?" "It really doesn't matter what they write, as long as you've got a young and beautiful piece of ass." "That must be a pretty picture; you dropping to your knees." "There was blood coming out of her eyes; coming out of her whatever." "Women. You have to treat them like s—t."

Grandiose-vs.-Vulnerable-Rage Pattern

As suggested in chapter 5, Trump may have the following pattern, associated with narcissistic personality disorder:

> [I]ndividuals with high NPI scores are highly invested in promoting their self-perceived superiority and are hypervigilant toward detecting and trying to diffuse potential threats to their grandiose self-perception.

You can point out his speech patterns as including self-promotion alternating with rageful criticism of others, even when it's because of his own decisions. Trump usually begins his rallies by talking about his high numbers, but he also brags about his money, his smart brain, his sexual potency. When something goes wrong, he wants to fight and blame others. He has a substantial history of treating many of his employees terribly. Here are just two examples:

> Trump said, "Who said to make this ceiling so low?" [at Trump Plaza]
> "You knew about this, Donald," Hyde replied. "We talked about it, if you remember, and the plans—"
> Abruptly Donald leaped up and punched his fist

through the tile. Then he turned on Hyde in a rage. . . . The tirade went on at great length as Trump "humiliated [Hyde] in front of twenty people, colleagues and professionals."

This incident is remarkable, not only the intensity of anger, but also the impulsiveness of punching his fist into the ceiling in front of twenty people. Ceilings are minor issues compared to dealing with world leaders, terrorist organizations, senators and representatives. It appears this is part of a pattern, rather than an isolated incident. Here's another example:

> O'Donnell finally reached his limit when Trump began to blame him for a series of crises that occurred around the opening of his biggest casino in Atlantic City, the Trump Taj Mahal. . . .
>
> Trump responded with a full-throated attack on O'Donnell's performance at the most profitable of his assets. . . .
>
> No longer able to endure Trump's self-righteous contempt and the continuous assaults on his character, O'Donnell resigned the very day.
>
> As Jack O'Donnell learned from painful experience, the Self-Righteous Narcissist will not listen to reason and is immune to arguments based on truth and logic.

This suggests the presence of a narrow pattern of behavior, since it has apparently happened many times in public (which hints at a lot more in private) and seems to fit the narcissistic pattern of grandiose promotion combined with vulnerable episodes of unmanaged emotions. This pattern of *grandiosity alternating with uncontrollable rages when his vulnerability is exposed* appears to have existed since childhood. He even admits he was sent by his parents to New York Military Academy to learn to manage his unruly character. When personality patterns exist from childhood, they rarely change as adults. They're like permanent teeth—you develop your adult personality mostly during your childhood.

Imagine Trump trying to calmly get through a day of difficult negotiations with members of Congress or world leaders or a Cuba Missile Crisis–type of standoff. Angry with a button.

These are some of the patterns you can tell potential voters or negative advocates about. Tell people to watch him and see how much of his speaking time at rallies, debates, and interviews is spent on emotional patterns and grandiose self-promotion combined with angry overreactions. Ask them to watch how much of the time he appears "presidential."

Telling Stories
One of the aspects of right-brain politics is that stories are far more appealing than factual data and logical reasoning (more left-brain stuff). Trump tells lots of stories, like the ones about Mexican immigrants being rapists and murderers. Sure, there are individual examples out of millions of people, but there are even more rapists and murderers among the white population of the United States because there are more whites. But that's numerical logic, which he has easily thrown out and his followers ignore.

He tells stories about thousands and thousands of Muslims celebrating the fall of the World Trade Center buildings on 9/11. The image of this is permanently planted in my brain, because it's a right-brain story—not because I believe it. Stories have that kind of power.

He tells the story of how he could shoot someone on Fifth Avenue in New York City, and he wouldn't lose any of his voters. Now that image is in my mind too, even though it is absurd. These are very subtle types of power that this man has for influencing people below the radar. I think even he is surprised at how powerful his manner of speaking can work, when it has a megaphone through Twitter and the media, and an audience with losses and resentments looking for an emotionally engaging leader who expresses some of their inner thoughts.

My suggestion is that you tell stories of the rise and fall of bubbles, like the dot-com bubble and the housing bubble and the stock market bubble. Tell people about *The Big Short* movie about the mortgage bubble that burst, and how millions and millions of people believed that house values would keep going up and that everyone's mortgage was in fine shape. Then the fall came—and few saw it in advance!

High-conflict politicians have the same pattern of rise and fall—we have history to prove it. Ask people: Don't you want to be one of the few who recognized the trump bubble early in 2016? Maybe he'll win the election or maybe he won't, but his bubble will burst someday—of that I am certain. I have seen it happen literally hundreds of times with high-conflict personalities. Let's hasten this process now and avoid the mess—and violence—that usually comes with it.

CONCLUSION

All put together, we are watching a bubble with Donald Trump. No one knows what he believes in and what he will do. He frequently and easily switches positions, which would be fatal to another candidate, but it doesn't harm him at all because of his patterns of speech and grandiose-vs.-vulnerable-rage pattern. His bubble is based on such intense emotion that the lack of substance just slips on by and is not a concern for his followers.

His one clear message (as was Hitler's) is that we should take action against people lower in the American dominance hierarchy, not the higher ups, such as Mexicans, Muslims, African Americans, women, and whomever else he chooses at the time. Without this focus, his "program" collapses. Ironically, many of Hitler's negative advocates, such a Putzi Hanfstaengl in chapter 7, said that they disagreed with Hitler on his hatred of the Jews, but he considered that only 5 percent of what Hitler was about, so he could tolerate that part. History has proven him wrong about the 5 percent—it was the cornerstone for Hitler.

Likewise, many of Trump's supporters believe that his racist and violent statements are just a minor part of who he is and something he will tone down after he gets elected. I asked the man I had the Trump discussion with earlier in this chapter if he thought Trump would actually build a wall. He said no, that Trump was just saying that to get attention and would back off from that after he gets elected. Of course, if he gets elected and if he's an HCP, he will increase his aggressive behavior rather than becoming more reasonable. That's why it's so important to explain the patterns of high-conflict politicians described in chapters 7 and 8 to Trump's supporters or potential negative advocates. Or just give them a copy of this book!

CHAPTER 10

RESTRAINING HIGH-CONFLICT POLITICIANS

(No More US against THEM—It's All of US Now)

Outwitted

He drew a circle that shut me out —
Heretic, rebel, a thing to flout.
Love and I had the wit to win
We drew a circle that took him in!

— Edwin Markham (1852–1940)

I **T BEARS REPEATING** that high-conflict people have a narrow pattern of *unrestrained aggressive behavior.* They can't stop themselves. They see all relationships as inherently adversarial. Their lives are filled with US-against-THEM behavior. They think that everyone is either a winner or a loser, so they have to prove that they are winners. This thinking and behavior doesn't go away on its own.

"But surely Trump knows he's acting badly."

"He's a smart person who is just saying and doing things to get elected."

"If he becomes president, he will shift into his responsible businessman mode and make smart, reasonable decisions."

"Trump will rely on smart, reasonable advisers and make sound decisions."

These are some of the things I hear in regard to Donald Trump. Fifteen years of experience tells me the opposite: Because of their narrow pattern of unrestrained aggressive behavior HCPs don't suddenly self-correct in a moment of insight and become reasonable and responsible. Forget about it! They have high-conflict personalities because they *don't* stop themselves.

IT'S UP TO US

Since they don't stop themselves, the larger community has to stop high-conflict people. If we don't, high-conflict leaders gain more power and become more aggressive, not more reasonable. We have seen this with many politicians over the past few years: disgraced mayors thrown out of office, errant governors removed, representatives and senators caught acting badly, as well as former presidents and many nations' dictators who have continued to act with unrestrained aggressive behavior until someone else stopped them.

LACK OF SELF-RESTRAINT

We have to understand that high-conflict personalities are different. I truly believe that Donald Trump does not realize his own power—he doesn't understand that his high-conflict speaking ability can unleash pure aggressive behavior in others. Remember the news report in the introduction to this book?

> The rancor is so blatant that Mr. Trump was asked about it during the debate on Thursday night in Miami. He said he had not seen the violent episode in Fayetteville, and when asked if he was encouraging his supporters' fury, he said, **"I hope not."**

I believe that Trump is simply speaking the way he has always spoken. This seems to be confirmed by news reporters who dealt with him in New York City over twenty years ago. Michael Grynbaum writes in the *New York Times:*

> Mr. Trump, over decades, honed the method of media management—cajoling, combating, at times dissembling—that he has unleashed, to potent effect, in this year's national campaign. Some Americans have been caught off guard by Mr. Trump's take-no-prisoners style, but New York's media veterans detect the old Trump playbook at work.

But is this a "playbook" that he can put down, or is this his personality? It doesn't seem as if he has changed a bit in decades. A pattern of behavior that doesn't change at all, even when it is self-defeating, demonstrates a personality problem rather than an optional playbook. It's embedded in his brain, regardless of his position in the world. The best example is that he hasn't changed a bit even now when he is running for the most responsible position in the world.

In short, he has a pattern of *unrestrained* verbal behavior that is exaggerated and risky—even to his chance to become president: "It's going to be a beautiful thing"; "China's killing us, just killing us"; "I could just punch him in the face"; "People like that used to be carried out on stretchers"; "You're incredible. I love you. I love you"; and so on. This pattern is so automatic that he lacks self-awareness of it and he will not be able to stop it, even if he wants to.

"Did you start World War III?" he may be asked someday. His answer will probably be: "I hope not!" Donald Trump lacks self-awareness of his own lack of self-restraint.

A LARGER LACK OF RESTRAINT

This lack of self-restraint goes beyond Trump. Since this is a book about any high-conflict politician, it's important to recognize these traits in other political candidates and in society at large. Not only do we need to educate people in order to stop trump bubbles from gaining power; we also have to become self-aware as a society about the dangers of lack of restraint and educate ourselves on what to do about it.

Over the past forty years, two other major trends have developed in the world driving people apart, rather than together. We are now producing more people with high-conflict personalities, such as Trump, and more high-conflict disputes, such as terrorism because of these trends:

1. Narcissism
2. Lack of restraint

These trends have gone hand in hand with our technological progress. Now we can be more narcissistic—self-centered as individuals—because our technological devices enable us to do much more on our own. We can work alone, live alone, have sex alone, believe whatever we want alone, make and keep lots of money almost on our own, and not care much about others anymore.

At the same time, governments have been removing restraints (laws and rules) that we used to have, which have made it easier to be innovative, to travel widely, to communicate much more rapidly, and to say anything we want in public. But also these moves have allowed some to make and keep lots of money for themselves, to be less accountable to others, to have media that is no longer restrained by the Fairness Doctrine (see our book *Splitting America*), and to have election laws that are unrestrained in the amount of money wealthy people can spend on candidates because of the Supreme Court's *Citizens United* decision (see *Splitting America*), and so forth.

At the same time, enabled by technological progress and removal of government restraints, modern media has been become much more aggressive and unrestrained in showing people's aggressive behavior: from sitcoms to bloody dramas to sexual explicitness to constant news of the world's worst behavior twenty-four hours a day, seven days a week.

I believe a turning point with this came in April 2007, when NBC News decided to air the self-made rant video of the Virginia Tech shooter after he killed more than thirty people. They said they struggled with making this decision, but I think they made a huge mistake—which helped set a trend: not only are we glorifying the violence, but we are now glorifying the *emotions without thinking* behind the violence. This type of brain-grabbing news demonstrates unrestrained aggressive behavior. And of course, YGMOWYPAT: you get more of what you pay attention to.

This combination is becoming dangerous. As you can see, it's a self-perpetuating perfect storm of lack of restraint:

Individuals growing up without self-restraint—essentially high-conflict people, including more personality disorders in society

Society removing restraints on aggressive behavior—largely under the guise of free speech and gun rights, which provide less freedom from fear

Media removing its self-restraint in showing more bad than good behavior

This is a spiral downward: More individuals with lack of self-restraint, who become politicians who pass laws allowing more lack of self-restraint, who enable media to promote more role models of lack of self-restraint, and on and on. While this all may be entertaining for adults, it's training for children and future leaders.

REAL PROBLEMS

I believe that narcissism and lack of restraint are the driving forces behind many of today's real problems. We need to address the following narcissistic trends by imposing more restraints, to bring us to a more realistic and modern balance of individualism *and* social responsibility—in other words individualism with less narcissism.

Narcissistic Wealth

Our culture of narcissism has created a fascination with stars rather than teamwork: athletic stars, movie stars, supermodels, Wall Street deal-makers, high-tech billionaires, and others who feel that they individually deserve amounts of money that are more than some countries' GNPs. This was not the case before 1970, when the spread between low and high income was much narrower and upward mobility was much more possible.

I remember one of my favorite baseball players, Stan Musial, who was offered a large bonus for his contribution to a winning season for the St. Louis Cardinals. He refused it and said it was teamwork that made the season and that there's no reason one player should make more than the others. By the end of the 1970s, with free agency and a new culture of deal-making, the opposite value was dominant as stars were born in many professions.

Along with this celebration of individuality and stardom has come a tolerance and enthusiasm for wealthy stars—on the stock market, on the Internet, and in the media. But this tolerance and encouragement for economic inequality has also brought a loss of community, humility, and teamwork—and greater fear and insecurity about the future for all. We need to rein in the extremes that we will tolerate, without stifling innovative free enterprise.

Political Narcissism

We have reached a time when everyone wants to be a leader and no one wants to follow. The large Republican pool of presidential candidates in 2016 helped create Donald Trump for president. So many candidates wanted to be the star—yet few, if any, demonstrated a strong ability to work with others and defer some of their own gratification for the good of the party or the nation.

They each tried to prove how strong and bossy they could be in replacing the federal government with their own individual wisdom. The Republican Party needs to re-examine its philosophy with or without Trump, the extreme version of this principle. It is always interesting to me when the prime stated goal of a candidate is that he or she can beat the other party's candidate, rather than serving the nation. These trends were part of the motivation for our book *Splitting America* in 2012. We need to put more restrictions on the polarization of parties, such as limiting their campaign seasons to six weeks (as some other successful democracies already do) and not allowing those with obviously toxic personalities to receive our party endorsements. There needs to be some minimum standards for our political leaders.

Religious and Cultural Narcissism

For a country based on religious freedom, established in our First Amendment, we are having a difficult time tolerating religious diversity. This has become a worldwide problem, as cultures have to learn how to share space with other cultures. The answers won't lie in disrespecting other cultures. While economic inequality appears to underlie much of the current resentment around the world, it often takes the form of religious and cultural warfare because that is such a large part of our human sense of identity and sense of community.

With subgroups of news media geared to each subgroup's prejudices, this narcissism is reinforced. Instead, we need to work to help individuals from different cultural and religious groups get together and learn about each other. Where this occurs, fewer high-conflict disputes are likely to happen.

TERRORISM

The appeal of terrorism to young people around the world seems based on trump bubbles as well. Over the Internet, recruiters tell young people how "beautiful" the ISIS Caliphate will be. Young male suicide bombers are promised seventy virgins in heaven. One wonders how they could believe that, yet it seems to be the same type of media images and hype that building Trump's "beautiful wall" is with Mexico. These are intense emotional messages without thinking.

Terrorism is, I believe, primarily the work of leaders with antisocial and narcissistic personality disorders who have no empathy for others, no remorse, and often have criminal histories. For example, former FBI profilers report that narcissistic personality disorder is notably present in terrorist leaders.

However, other than the narcissistic psychopaths, terrorists are mostly followers who have many of the same losses and resentments that we are seeing in the United States: economic inequality, exclusion from peaceful political processes, and feelings of religious and cultural disrespect. If we expect to rein in the violent behaviors they are spawning, we will need to address these issues with more *empathy, attention, and respect* than we have in the past.

Young people in the Middle East have similar anger and frustrations to those in the United States, as reporter George Packer discovered in Tunisia:

> A friend of Mohamed's, an unemployed telecommunications engineer named Nabil Selliti, left Douar Hicher [a poor suburb of Tunis in Tunisia] to fight in Syria. Oussama Romdhani, who edits the *Arab Weekly* in Tunis, told me that in the Arab world the most likely radicals are people in technical or scientific fields who lack the kind of humanities education that fosters critical thought. Before

Selliti left, Mohamed asked him why he was going off to fight. Selliti replied, "I can't build anything in this country. But the Islamic State gives us the chance to create, to build bombs, to use technology." In July 2013, Selliti blew himself up in a suicide bombing in Iraq.

The reality is much more complicated than blaming it all on Islamic fundamentalism. Many of the terrorists actually have little knowledge of Islam. Packer spoke with another young man, Kamal, who wanted to be a police officer. But unable to get such a job, he drifted toward ISIS. It had more to do with "an expression of rage, not of ideology." In his poor community, "anger was enough to send young people off to fight."

"The youth are lost," Kamal told me. "There's no justice. . . . If you want to stop terrorism, then bring good schools, bring transportation—because the roads are terrible—and bring jobs for young people, so that Douar Hicher becomes like the parts of Tunisia where you Westerners come to have fun."

Terrorism is the result of unaddressed real economic problems in the Middle East, just like Trumpism is the result of unaddressed real economic problems for the young white lower-middle class in the United States. We need to become more self-aware of our part in allowing these problems to develop and to exist largely unrecognized.

We also need to realize that science without humanities *contributes to trump bubbles without thought.* Just like the mechanical brilliance Robert McNamara and others demonstrated in our war against Vietnam, which McNamara later regretted. (See the 2004 Academy Award-winning documentary: *The Fog of War: Eleven Lessons from the Life of Robert S. McNamara.*) Economics and education can make a big difference for young people around the world. These are real problems, not bad religions.

We have to change our rhetoric from attacking those around

the world for their religions and cultures, and instead join with the large majority of people and isolate the few terrorist leaders for the narcissistic psychopaths that they are. Otherwise, our own US-against-THEM culture is feeding their US-against-THEM culture.

A CULTURE OF ALL OF US

Over twenty years ago, marriage researchers John and Julie Gottman discovered that healthy marriages have a 5:1 ratio of positive comments and interactions to negative ones. In other words, you can have criticisms, freedom of expression, and rude behavior—but only if you have five times more positive communication and behavior overall. If you want to maintain a healthy relationship, you need to have a sustainable balance.

In today's high-conflict culture, we are fast losing our ability to sustain a healthy national relationship. With daily hostile political speech for a presidential campaign that began at least eighteen months before the November 2016 elections, we easily have had an unhealthy 5:1 ratio of negative to positive statements and interactions blasted by the media 24/7. It is extremely toxic for the nation.

As Donald Saposnek and I wrote in *Splitting America*: "We are, after all, the American family. It's up to us!" And it is possible to be US again—all of US—by learning and reinforcing collaborative skills.

COLLABORATIVE SKILLS

Over the past two decades, there has been a trend in many professions toward collaboration. This has happened concurrently in law, education, health care, science, and other fields, without much knowledge of what the other professions are doing. In the high-conflict dispute resolution field (negotiation and mediation), collaborative skills are a big part of the solution. This is a very satisfying trend to me, worth much more in human relations than in financial gain. I believe we are rediscovering our humanity.

But this means that we need to learn new skills of problem-solving and cooperation. Those are some of the skills we learn and teach with our High Conflict Institute trainings, books, and videos:

How to calm yourself in a conflict

How to disagree on substance and ideas without making personal attacks

How to communicate with *empathy, attention,* and *respect (EAR statements)*

How to write BIFF emails that are *brief, informative, friendly,* and *firm*

How to make and respond to proposals respectfully

How to set limits on bad behavior in a respectful way

These are the types of skills I believe America needs at this point in time to solve problems together and avoid creating more problems unnecessarily. People who have reasonable self-restraint can work together collaboratively and be much more powerful together. We need leaders who value everyone's perspective and ideas, such as we see in many areas of business, communities that work well, and political problem-solving at smaller levels, such as the cities and states that are thriving. We don't need leadership that demonstrates arrogance, a lack of empathy, and bullying to solve problems.

Keep in mind that collaboration among many countries was what helped rebuild Germany after World War II and put it on a dynamic economic course that still lasts today. Let's skip World War III and instead go to work to solve these problems together now.

MY PREDICTIONS

Donald Trump is not a collaborative leader. He is headed in exactly the opposite direction from real modern solutions to real modern problems. His US-against-THEM rhetoric will produce one of the three following scenarios:

The Republican Party will recognize his dangerous patterns and select another candidate at their convention in July 2016. (This book came out in time to help in that effort.) He will seek revenge, sue the Republican Party, and keep a significant part of the electorate angry at "the establishment," rather than helping with any reconciliation effort. He will not organize a third-party run—that would be too much work. He really wants to be president, but he doesn't want to do the work of getting there. It's not in his personality.

If he is the Republican candidate, he will brutally attack the Democratic candidate with personal criticisms, false information, and daily chaos. If he's lucky, there will be one to two terrorist events on U.S. soil right before the election—perhaps in retaliation for his endless rhetoric against Muslims—that he will turn to his advantage to win the election. However, if he's not lucky and the truth about his patterns becomes a focus of attention, he will lose the election. If it's a narrow loss, he will demand a recount and keep the country in chaos (unlike Al Gore in 2000). If it's a bigger loss, he will seek revenge by suing the Republican Party and keeping a significant part of the electorate angry at "the establishment," rather than helping with any reconciliation effort. Rather than quietly keeping a low profile (like George W. Bush did after Barack Obama followed him into office), Trump will share his criticizing thoughts every day on Twitter and with other eager media.

If he becomes the president of the United States, within twelve months we will be at war with somebody. He tends to inspire violence and lack of restraint—which leads to lack of physical restraint, which leads to organized aggressive behavior, which leads inevitably to war. He will "split" the world into allies and enemies. We will have more chaos than we do now in the Middle East— and on American soil. Friends and family members will start hating each other, and schoolchildren will become disrespectful and violent toward people who look different from them.

I hope I'm wrong about this.

Thinking people need to speak up and tell everyone, including Trump's followers and potential negative advocates, that they share their concerns and their problems. Their needs are important and should be represented in Washington by leaders who can work with other leaders to address the real issues. Let them know that Trump's answers of US against THEM are bubbles that will solve nothing and create dangerous levels of conflict where collaborative solutions would have been possible.

CONCLUSION

A trump bubble can be a politician, a policy, or a war when emotions trump thinking in politics. When fear trumps facts. When leader love trumps logic.

We've reached a point in history when we are creating many of our own problems and don't realize it until severe damage is done. It's easy to get too emotionally excited about an idea in the present and stop thinking about the consequences. Our modern communications explosion has encouraged this, inundating us with dramatic images of war and devastation—from around the world in real time. There's some good information but a lot of bad information going viral on the Internet. These trends need more self-restraint by the media and all of us who love to watch.

We have learned over the past one hundred years that our technological advances, our proliferation of media, and our freedom of movement can also create conflicts that won't be resolved with all-or-nothing, US-against-THEM solutions. Europe learned this after two disastrous world wars.

Our brains have two hemispheres: one more capable of analytical problem-solving and the other more capable of defensive, all-or-nothing quick reactions. Focusing only on emotions or only on analysis puts us out of balance. We need new ideas and we need to protect ourselves and keep our stability grounded in useful traditions. We need to use our whole brains, not just half a brain. A community with a good liberal and conservative balance can be brilliant and enduring. In many ways, that has been the history of the United States. But maintaining balance is a delicate process.

The relatively new twin problems of narcissism and lack of restraint require a new balance. "Pure" politics are tempting, but a failure. Hitler attempted to develop a pure race of Germans and it destroyed much of Europe and millions of people's lives. ISIS is trying to create a pure religious culture and it is leading to their own destruction, as countries around the world rein them in with their far-superior numbers and strength. Fox News is attempting to develop pure conservative politics and in the process it may be destroying the Republican Party.

All modern media is pulling us toward the excitement of US-against-THEM. That's because it's the basis of drama. But politics is more important than drama. A little boredom can be a good thing, if it means that people and politicians are learning to get along. There's no rule that politicians have to be entertainers and blamers. This US-against-THEM approach is the problem, not the solution.

When an organization or community is out of balance, more high-conflict people rise up and you get more trump bubbles in leadership. In a sense, they point where you need to go. At this time in politics, we need to go toward less-narcissistic politicians and increase our social restraints.

Perhaps we should have a shorter campaign season, as some countries have, to reduce the "circus" of TV debates and grandstanding. Perhaps we should restrain what they can say as candidates—have some minimum standards of civility for our country's highest office. Perhaps we should return to the Fairness Doctrine, where news programs are required to air more than one point of view, so that the emotions of one group don't become isolated from reality in ways that endanger the world.

Perhaps we should refuse to watch the news programs that glorify personal attacks and false statements. Remember YGMOWYPAT: You get more of what you pay attention to.

It appears that high-conflict people are increasing in society. Until we figure out how to restrain high-conflict politicians, we will get more trump bubbles. Solving this problem is no longer up to THEM. It's up to all of US. And now, it's up to you!

REFERENCES

INTRODUCTION: HIGH-CONFLICT POLITICIANS

As Dorothy Thompson: Nagorski, A. 2012. *Hitlerland: American Eyewitnesses to the Nazi Rise to Power.* New York: Simon & Schuster, 85.

Friday, March 11: Parker, A. 2016. "Riskiest Political Act of 2016? Protesting at Rallies for Donald Trump." *New York Times,* March 10.

CHAPTER 1: RIGHT-BRAIN POLITICS

[The Republican Party's] most prominent guardians: Barbaro, M., A. Parker, and J. Martin. 2016. "Rank and File Republicans Tell Party Elites: We're Sticking with Donald Trump." *New York Times,* March 4.

In 1932, Edward Mowrer: Nagorski, A. 2012. *Hitlerland: American Eyewitnesses to the Nazi Rise to Power.* New York: Simon & Schuster, 100.

Emotions and Logic: Numerous brain researchers identify these general differences in the right and left hemisphere, while cautioning that there is some overlap. These are just a few of my sources for this information:

Damasio, A. 1999. *The Feeling of What Happens: Body and Emotion in the Making of Consciousness.* New York: Harcourt, Brace & Company.

Doidge, N. 2007. *The Brain That Changes Itself.* New York: Penguin Books.

Schore, A. 2003. *Affect Regulation and the Repair of the Self.* New York: W. W. Norton & Company.

Schore, Allan. 2012. *The Science of the Art of Psychotherapy.* New York: W. W. Norton & Company.

Seigel, D. 1999. *The Developing Mind.* New York: Guilford Press.

Seigel, D. 2007. *The Mindful Brain.* New York: W. W. Norton & Company.

The Amygdala: Goleman, D. 1995. *Emotional Intelligence: Why It Can Matter More Than IQ.* New York: Bantam Books.

Goleman, D. 2006. *Social Intelligence: The New Science of Human Relationships.* New York: Bantam Books.

The Larger Right Amygdala: Kanai, R., T. Feilden, C. Firth, and G. Rees. 2011. "Political Orientations Are Correlated with Brain Structure in Young Adults." *Current Biology* 21 (8): 677–80, April 26. Retrieved March 15, 2016 from http://www.cell.com/current-biology/fulltext/S0960-9822(11)00289-2.

Inborn or Learned Differences: Haidt, J. 2012. *The Righteous Mind: Why Good People Are Divided By Politics and Religion.* New York: Vintage Books, 324–29.

CHAPTER 2: LEADER LOVE
(THE SEDUCTION OF US AGAINST THEM)

There were those who met Hitler: Nagorski, A. 2012. *Hitlerland: American Eyewitnesses to the Nazi Rise to Power.* New York: Simon & Schuster, 3–4.

What Trump is doing: Douthat, R. 2016. "The Elements of Trumpism." *New York Times,* March 5.

Our faith in the value of leadership: Rothman, J. 2016. "Shut Up and Sit Down: Why the Leadership Industry Rules." *New Yorker.* February 29, 64.

Anthropologists say that we human beings: Exhibit at the American Museum of Natural History, New York, April 2015.

Moral psychologist: Haidt, J. 2012. *The Righteous Mind: Why Good People Are Divided by Politics and Religion.* New York: Vintage Books, 100.

Consider a test of whether: Sunstein, C., and R. Hastie. 2014. *Wiser: Getting Beyond Groupthink to Make Groups Smarter.* Boston: Harvard Business Review Press, 86.

There could be no question about the German people: Nagorski, *Hitlerland,* 175.

And this intoxication made them blind: Nagorski, *Hitlerland,* 259.

He was male in his early thirties: Nagorski, *Hitlerland,* 148.

Transfixed, as if in some devotional ecstasy: Nagorski, *Hitlerland,* 35.

CHAPTER 3: THE POWER OF LOSS AND RESENTMENT

The intersection of inequality: Edsall, T. 2016. "Why Trump Now?" *New York Times,* March 1. (Quoting Jared Bernstein of the Center for Budget and Policy Priorities explaining "disillusionment with old guard Republicans")

Dominance hierarchy: Grandin, T. 2005. *Animals in Translation.* New York: Harcourt Books.

Relative deprivation: Cassidy, J. 2006. "Relatively Deprived: How Poor Is Poor?" *New Yorker,* April 3, 42–47.

Charles Murray describes: Murray, C. 2016. "Trump's America," *Wall Street Journal,* February 12.

The widespread sense that all the elites: Edsall, T. "Why Trump Now?" *New York Times,* March 1.

The core theme of the Republican establishment: Edsall, "Why Trump Now?"

There are more Mexicans leaving: Brooks, D. 2016. "A Little Reality on Immigration." *New York Times,* February 19.

CHAPTER 4: THE POWER OF EMOTIONAL MEDIA

Liberals and conservatives actually move further apart: Haidt, J. 2012. *The Righteous Mind: Why Good People Are Divided by Politics and Religion.* New York: Vintage Books, 100.

Conflict is intrinsically more interesting: Sherman, G. 2014. *The Loudest Voice in the Room.* New York: Random House, 7.

Play, concerts and movies: Goleman, D. 2006. *Social Intelligence: The New Science of Human Relationships.* New York: Bantam Books, 48.

Despite pre-event disclaimers: Parker, A. 2016. "Riskiest Political Act of 2016? Protesting at Rallies for Donald Trump." *New York Times,* March 10.

With the advent of cable news: Eddy, B., and D. Saposnek. 2012. *Splitting America: How Politicians, Super PACs and the News Media Mirror High Conflict Divorce.* Scottsdale, AZ: High Conflict Institute Press.

As a pugnacious television adviser: Sherman, *Loudest Voice in the Room,* 5.

Now Obama advisers were getting word: Sherman, *Loudest Voice in the Room,* 319.

In a meeting at Fox News: Sherman, *Loudest Voice in the Room,* 9.

Antipolitics: Brooks, D. 2016. "The Governing Cancer of Our Time." *New York Times,* February 26.

Why are whites overdosing: Cherlin, A. 2016. "Why Are Whites Death Rates Rising?" *New York Times.* February 22.

CHAPTER 5: THE POWER OF PERSONALITY

The crowd went wild: Range, P. 2016. *1924: The Year That Made Hitler.* New York: Little, Brown and Company, 77.

Then the stock market crashed: Nagorski, A. 2012. *Hitlerland: American Eyewitnesses to the Nazi Rise to Power.* New York: Simon & Schuster, 71.

Their experiences and observations: Nagorski, *Hitlerland,* 324.

A lot of Trump's momentum: Lepore, J. 2016. "Crying Trump." *New Yorker,* March 8.

Traits of narcissistic personality disorder: American Psychiatric Association: *Diagnostic and Statistical Manual of Mental Disorders,* Fifth Edition. Arlington, VA, American Psychiatric Association, 2013.

[I]ndividuals with high NPI scores: Cain, N. et al. 2008. "Narcissism at the Crossroad." *Clinical Psychology Review* 28, 638–56.

Here is a list of predictions: Eddy, B. 2016. "Personality Awareness Skills." *High Conflict Institute & Unhooked Books Monthly Report,* February.

Leadership and Manipulation: Regier, N. *Leadership and Manipulation: Donald Trump Case Study, Part 1.* Retrieved March 16, 2016 from http://next-element.com/leadership-and-manipulation-donald-trump-case-study-part-1/.

Regier, N. *Leadership and Manipulation: Donald Trump Case Study, Part 2.* Retrieved March 18, 2016 from http://next-element.com/leadership-and-manipulation-donald-trump-case-study-part-2/.

His foreign policy plans included: Lepore, "Crying Trump."

Bernie [Sanders] and Hillary: Bethea, C. 2016. "Word of the Day: Stumped." *New Yorker.* April 11.

He knew how to tap into: Nagorski, *Hitlerland,* 324.

CHAPTER 6: SPLITTING AMERICA IN HALF

Splitting is unconscious: Eddy, B., and D. Saposnek. 2012. *Splitting America: How Politicians, Super PACs and the News Media Mirror High Conflict Divorce.* Scottsdale, AZ: High Conflict Institute Press, 32.

Fred Trump, Donald's father: Burgo, J. 2015. *The Narcissist You Know: Defending Yourself Against Extreme Narcissists in an All-About-Me Age.* New York: Touchstone, 173.

"Staff splitting," . . . is a much: Linehan, M. 1993. *Cognitive-Behavioral Treatment of Borderline Personality Disorder.* New York: Guilford Press, 431.

Based on 2014 data: *A Deep Dive into Party Affiliation.* April 7, 2015. Retrieved March 19, 2016 from http://www.e.org/2015/04/07/a-deep-dive-into-party-affiliation/. (Referring to data gathered by the Pew Research Center.)

Voters are increasingly divided: Grier, P. 2015. "Twilight of the 'Floater Voter.'" *Christian Science Monitor,* December 14.

CHAPTER 7: HIGH-CONFLICT POLITICIANS AND THEIR PREDICTABLE WARS

The impression I gained: Nagorski, A. 2012. *Hitlerland: American Eyewitnesses to the Nazi Rise to Power.* New York: Simon & Schuster, 81.

Everybody in Germany knows: Nagorski, *Hitlerland,* 99.

German troops had reached: Nagorski, *Hitlerland,* 312.

Joseph McCarthy was: Karnow, S. 1984. *Vietnam: A History.* New York: Penguin Books, 185.

Senator McCarthy: Karnow, *Vietnam,* 374.

Nixon's crusade against: Karnow, *Vietnam,* 593.

In 1953, his father got him: Caro, R. A. 2012. *The Years of Lyndon Johnson: The Passage of Power.* New York: Vintage Books, 64.

In 2003, 4,000 pages: Frommer, F. 2003. "Hearing Transcripts Show McCarthy's Bully Tactics." *San Diego Union-Tribune.* May 6.

Johnson especially feared: Karnow, *Vietnam,* 336.

Subsequent research: Karnow, *Vietnam,* 336.

Opinion polls showed: Karnow, *Vietnam,* 390.

He now mobilized two men: Karnow, *Vietnam,* 390.

People with great credibility: Karnow, *Vietnam,* 361.

That primitive bluster: Karnow, *Vietnam,* 337–38.

CHAPTER 8: THE IRAQ WAR BUBBLE AND BEYOND

The [order] formally disbanded: Bush, G. W. 2010. *Decision Points.* New York: Random House, 262.

She was forty-four years old: Heilemann, J., and M. Halperin. 2010. *Game Change: Obama and the Clintons, McCain and Palin, and the Race of a Lifetime.* New York: HarperCollins, 359.

"You know what they say the difference": Heilemann and Halperin, *Game Change,* 372.

Donations and Volunteers: Heilemann and Halperin, *Game Change,* 373.

Ailes, watching the Republican convention: Sherman, G. 2014. *The Loudest Voice in the Room.* New York: Random House, 325.

Partly because of her: Sherman, *Loudest Voice in the Room,* 321.

Hiring Palin brought: Sherman, *Loudest Voice in the Room,* 322.

Ailes began to doubt: Sherman, *Loudest Voice in the Room,* 324.

This is in stark contrast: Caro, R. A. 2012. *The Years of Lyndon Johnson: The Passage of Power.* New York: Vintage Books, 64.

Likewise, the unified force: Meacham, J.. 2015. *Destiny and Power: The American Odyssey of George Herbert Walker Bush.* New York: Random House.

In January 1991: Karnow, S. 1984. *Vietnam: A History.* New York: Penguin Books, 15.

CHAPTER 9: TALKING WITH TRUMP BUBBLE SUPPORTERS

Morality binds and blinds: Haidt, J. 2012. *The Righteous Mind: Why Good People Are Divided by Politics and Religion.* New York: Vintage Books, 366.

There were those American reporters: Nagorski, A. 2012. *Hitlerland: American Eyewitnesses to the Nazi Rise to Power.* New York: Simon & Schuster, 3-4.

As Hitler talked about: Nagorski, *Hitlerland,* 35.

Look at that face: Corasaniti, N., and M. Haberman. "Barrage of Attack Ads Threaten to Undermine Donald Trump." 2016. *New York Times,* April 11.

[I]ndividuals with high NPI scores: Cain, N. et al. 2008. "Narcissism at the Crossroad." *Clinical Psychology Review* 28, 638–56.

Fred Trump, Donald's father: Burgo, J. 2015. *The Narcissist You Know: Defending Yourself Against Extreme Narcissists in an All-About-Me Age.* New York: Touchstone, 173.

Trump said, "Who said: Burgo, *Narcissist You Know,* 224.

O'Donnell finally reached his limit: Burgo, *Narcissist You Know,* 225.

CHAPTER 10: RESTRAINING HIGH-CONFLICT POLITICIANS

Mr. Trump over decades: Grynbaum, M. M. 2016. "Donald Trump and New York Tabloids Pick Their Elaborate Dance Back Up." *New York Times,* April 11.

Terrorism is, I believe: Navarro, J. 2005. *Hunting Terrorists: A Look at the Psychopathology of Terror.* Springfield, IL: Charles C. Thomas.

A friend of Mohamed's: Packer, G. 2016. "Exporting Jihad: The Arab Spring Has Given Tunisians the Freedom to Act on Their Unhappiness." *New Yorker,* March 28, 40.

"The youth are lost": Packer, "Exporting Jihad," 41.

Over twenty years ago: Gottman, J. 1994. *Why Marriages Succeed or Fail: And How You Can Make Yours Last.* New York: Simon & Schuster.

ACKNOWLEDGEMENTS

I want to thank my wife, Alice, for her insight, encouragement and critical feedback as I tackled this project in a very short period of time. She is almost always right about what needs to be added and what needs to be subtracted from my writing ideas.

Megan Hunter gets lots of credit for not only publishing this challenging book, but for working on an extremely tight schedule. It has been so exciting to work almost seamlessly with her, so that there is no wasted effort or time in producing important and timely information for our readers and the general public. I also appreciate my sister-in-law Cathy for her ongoing edits and feedback when I wrote the first draft of this book as a daily blog. And my literary advisor, Scott Edelstein, deserves credit for guiding me throughout my writing and publishing efforts over the past several years.

I want to thank my team at High Conflict Institute—our staff and trainers—for inspiring me every day and helping me believe that I have something to offer. I am constantly learning from you: Michelle, Diane, Trissan, Sue, John, Georgi, Michael, Shawn, Tammy, Debbie, Tracey and Andrea. There are many friends and others who have worked with us and taught me and helped refine our ideas for working with high-conflict people with empathy, attention and respect. I thank you all.

Lastly, I want to thank my editor, Catherine Broberg, who has joined in the accelerated pace of this book by editing it on a very tight timeline. I almost always accept her edits and appreciate her many writing tips. It is a great experience to work with such skilled colleagues! And many thanks to Julian Leon for the exuberant cover of this book! He got the tone just right!

ABOUT THE AUTHOR

William A. ("Bill") Eddy is an attorney, therapist, mediator, and president of the High Conflict Institute based in San Diego, California. Mr. Eddy provides training to professionals worldwide on the subject of managing high-conflict personalities. He has provided seminars to attorneys, mediators, judges, mental health professionals, human resource professionals, employee assistance professionals, ombuds, hospital and university administrators, government officials, law enforcement, homeowners' association managers, and others. He has presented in over thirty states, several provinces in Canada, as well as in France, Sweden, Austria, Australia, and New Zealand.

As an attorney, he is a certified family law specialist in California, where he has represented clients in family court for fifteen years and provided divorce mediation services for over twenty years. Prior to that, he provided psychotherapy for twelve years to children, adults, couples, and families in psychiatric hospitals and outpatient clinics as a licensed clinical social worker.

He taught Negotiation and Mediation at the University of San Diego School of Law for six years. He is currently the senior family mediator at the National Conflict Resolution Center in San Diego, California. He is a part-time faculty member at the Pepperdine University School of Law, where he has taught the Psychology of Conflict for four years, and a part-time faculty member of the National Judicial College. For the past several years, he has also provided an online CEU course for mental health professionals titled "Working with High Conflict Personalities."

He has provided consultation and training on workplace issues to Intel, San Diego Navy Medical Center, Mt. Royal University, Social Security Administrative Law Judges, U.S. National

Merit Protection System Board Administrative Law Judges, the State Services Authority in Melbourne, Australia, and many other organizations.

In 2008, he developed the C.A.R.S. Method of Conflict Resolution, for managing high-conflict people in workplace conflict, neighbor disputes, and family disputes. In 2009, he wrote a workbook and manual for the New Ways for Families method of assisting potentially high-conflict parents in separation and divorce in family courts. He also developed the New Ways for Mediation method, which includes providing a strong structure and reinforcing negotiation skills for clients to use during the process—especially designed for managing high-conflict people so that they can reach agreements. In 2014 he co-developed the New Ways for Work method with L. Georgi DiStefano, LCSW, which is based on conflict resolution skills training for potentially high-conflict employees and managers.

He obtained his law degree in 1992 from the University of San Diego, a master of social work degree in 1981 from San Diego State University, and a bachelor's degree in psychology in 1970 from Case Western Reserve University.

Bill Eddy's websites:
www.HighConflictInstitute.com
www.BIFFresponse.com
www.NewWays4Families.com

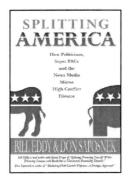

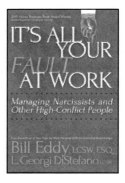

CPSIA information can be obtained at www.ICGtesting.com
Printed in the USA
LVOW10s1040190516

489017LV00001B/1/P